SpringerBriefs in Computer Science

SpringerBriefs present concise summaries of cutting-edge research and practical applications across a wide spectrum of fields. Featuring compact volumes of 50 to 125 pages, the series covers a range of content from professional to academic.

Typical topics might include:

- A timely report of state-of-the art analytical techniques
- A bridge between new research results, as published in journal articles, and a contextual literature review
- A snapshot of a hot or emerging topic
- An in-depth case study or clinical example
- A presentation of core concepts that students must understand in order to make independent contributions

Briefs allow authors to present their ideas and readers to absorb them with minimal time investment. Briefs will be published as part of Springer's eBook collection, with millions of users worldwide. In addition, Briefs will be available for individual print and electronic purchase. Briefs are characterized by fast, global electronic dissemination, standard publishing contracts, easy-to-use manuscript preparation and formatting guidelines, and expedited production schedules. We aim for publication 8–12 weeks after acceptance. Both solicited and unsolicited manuscripts are considered for publication in this series.

**Indexing: This series is indexed in Scopus, Ei-Compendex, and zbMATH **

John Lawrence Nazareth

Concise Guide to Numerical Algorithmics

The Foundations and Spirit of Scientific Computing

Springer

John Lawrence Nazareth
University of Washington
Seattle, WA, USA

ISSN 2191-5768 ISSN 2191-5776 (electronic)
SpringerBriefs in Computer Science
https://doi.org/10.1007/978-3-031-21762-3

This Springer imprint is published by the registered company Springer Nature Switzerland AG
The registered company address is: Gewerbestrasse 11, 6330 Cham, Switzerland
(www.springernature.com/mycopy)

Dedicated, with grateful thanks, to my mentors,
George Dantzig, William Davidon,
Stuart Dreyfus, and Beresford Parlett,
who, as time went by, also became friends

Preface

Mathematics in full-flower as we know it today, both pure and applied, has evolved from the root concept of number. Likewise, the foundation of modern computer science is the concept of the symbol-based algorithm. The central theme of this book is that these two foundational concepts—number and algorithm—can be brought together in two fundamentally different ways.

The first approach, speaking metaphorically, is to bring "algorithm under the rubric of number." This leads to the well-established discipline of *numerical analysis*, which today is fully embraced by pure and applied mathematics and has widespread applications in science and engineering. (It might have been preferable to call this discipline "algorithmic numerics," but traditional nomenclature must now prevail.)

The second approach, again speaking metaphorically, is the converse, namely, to bring "number under the rubric of algorithm." This leads to a re-emerging discipline within computer science to which the name *numerical algorithmic science and engineering (NAS&E)*, or more compactly, *numerical algorithmics*, will be attached. A discussion of the underlying rationale for numerical algorithmics, its foundational models of computation, its organizational details, and its role, in conjunction with numerical analysis, in support of the modern modus operandi of scientific computing, or computational science and engineering, is the primary focus of this short monograph.

Our book comprises six chapters, each with its own bibliography. Chapters 2, 3 and 6 present its primary content. Chapters 1, 4, and 5 are briefer, and they provide contextual material for the three primary chapters and smooth the transition between them. An outline of each chapter now follows.

Chapter 1 is titled "The Big Picture: Mathematics, Science and Engineering" and it sets the stage for subsequent chapters of the book. The primary content of this book—the concepts of number and algorithm and their integration to recreate the discipline of numerical algorithmics within computer science—is placed into its broader context of mathematics, science and engineering. A "visual icon" is presented which captures the relationships between these three broad, embracing arenas and their modi operandi. It serves to frame the discussion in this chapter and, in particular, it enables us to clarify the nomenclature, or terminology, used throughout our book.

Although every schoolchild today learns number representation and the basic arithmetic operations on decimals at an early age, the *concept of a fully-symbolized number itself* is far from elementary. This is the topic of Chap. 2, which is titled "Number: The Language of Science." We will begin with a discussion of symbolization in human language and then proceed to the symbolization of number. Mathematicians have developed a proper understanding of the latter and of resulting *number systems* only quite recently during the past four centuries. We will discuss some of these number systems, namely, cardinal integers, signed integers, rationals, and reals, and their *symbolic* representation using different bases. We present historical background and contrast symbol-based vis-à-vis magnitude-based representation of numbers. We conclude with the observation that the structure that underlies the foregoing basic number systems was subsequently extended, generalized, or relaxed, leading to other systems of numbers, for example, complex, algebraic, and hyperreal, and to numerous other key mathematical concepts, thereby evolving over time into the highly-elaborated mathematics of today. (Our foregoing metaphorical phrase, "under the rubric of number," refers to this overarching umbrella of mathematics.)

Chapter 3 is titled "Algorithmics: The Spirit of Computing" and it presents the fundamental notion of an algorithm, our focus here being on its traditional, "symbol-based" conception. We will describe a selected set of formal models of an algorithm and universal computer in a non-traditional and novel manner. These and other formal models are the *theoretical foundation* of the discipline of computer science—the so-called "grand unified theory of computation"—which was developed by mathematical logicians during the 1930s, before the advent of the electronic, digital computer in the mid-1940s. During the early days of the ensuing computer revolution, numerical computation was paramount, and its *practical foundation* was the finite-precision, floating-point model. This model was developed by numerical analysts, who played a leading role in the creation of the discipline of computer science, and it is the topic of the next section of this chapter. Finally, just as the basic number concept led to the development of much broader number systems, so did the basic concept of a symbol-based algorithm lead to the much broader conception of *algorithmic systems* for computation, for example, neural, quantum, and natural, as is briefly itemized in the concluding section. (Again our foregoing metaphorical phrase, "under the rubric of algorithm," refers to the overarching umbrella of computer science.)

Before we turn to a synthesis of number and algorithm as presented in the previous two chapters, we briefly consider the numerical problems that must themselves be solved in practice. This is the topic of Chap. 4, titled "A Taxonomy of Numerical Problems." As in Chap. 1, we again use a visual form of presentation, premised on four key partitions of the variables, parameters, and structural characteristics of the numerical problems under consideration: infinite vis-à-vis finite dimensional; continuous vis-à-vis discrete; deterministic vis-à-vis stochastic; defined by networks/graphs vis-à-vis not defined by such structures. This taxonomy enables us to highlight the distinction between numerical analysis within mathematics and numerical algorithmics within computer science. It is premised on the key observation that the great "watershed" in numerical computation is much more between infinite-dimensional and finite-dimensional numerical problems than it is between continuous and discrete numerical problems.

Chapter 5, which is titled "Numerical Analysis: Algorithm Under the Rubric of Number," is again ancillary and gives a brief overview of this discipline, now well established within mathematics, both pure and applied. We outline its theoretical foundation, which is provided by the landmark Blum-Cucker-Shub-Smale (BCSS) model of computation, and its practical foundations, based on the IEEE 754, finite-precision, floating-point standardization and the more recently-proposed Chebfun model.

Chapter 6 titled "Numerical Algorithmics: Number Under the Rubric of Algorithm" is the third main chapter of this book and it is premised on the previous discussion in Chaps. 2 and 3, with its broader context provided by the other, earlier chapters. We begin with a definition of this re-emerging discipline within computer science and a discussion of its underlying rationale. Real-number models of computation in the Turing tradition, which form the theoretical foundation for numerical algorithmics, are briefly surveyed. We then turn to the practical foundations of this discipline, and, in particular, we contrast the standard floating-point model and a newly-introduced "unum-posit" model. The content and organization of numerical algorithmics (NAS&E) is discussed in detail. The complementary disciplines of numerical analysis, headquartered within mathematics, and numerical algorithmics (NAS&E), headquartered within computer science, can provide an effective platform for the investigation of the problems and models of science and engineering by means of the modern computer, a modus operandi that is known today as scientific computing, or computational science and engineering.

Mathematical formalism has been kept to a minimum, and, whenever possible, we have sought to employ visual and verbal forms of presentation, and to make the discussion entertaining and readable—*an extended essay* on the foundations and spirit of our subject matter—through the use of motivating quotations and illustrative examples. Direct quotations from sources are often clarified through insertions within [square brackets] and through the use of *italics*. And the titles of referenced works are explicitly included within the text in order to minimize the need to look them up within the bibliography attached to each chapter.

Nevertheless, this book is not intended for the general reader. The reader is expected to have a working knowledge of the basics of computer science, an exposure to basic linear algebra and calculus (and perhaps some real analysis), and an understanding of elementary mathematical concepts such as convexity of sets and functions, networks and graphs, and so on.

Although this book is not suitable for use as the principal textbook for a course on numerical algorithmics (NAS&E), it will be of value as a supplementary reference for a variety of courses. It can also serve as the primary text for a research seminar. And it can be recommended for self-study of the foundations and organization of NAS&E to graduate and advanced undergraduate students with sufficient mathematical maturity and a background in computing. For a more technical accompaniment to this essay, one that is an embodiment of *numerical algorithmic science* within the context of a particular numerical problem area, see Nazareth [1], *The Newton-Cauchy Framework: A Unified Approach to Unconstrained Nonlinear Minimization.* And, likewise, for a more technical accompaniment and embodiment of *numerical algorithmic engineering,* again for a particular application area, see Nazareth [2], *DLP and Extensions: An Optimization Model and Decision Support System.*

When departments of computer science were first created within universities worldwide during the middle of the last century, numerical analysis was an important part of the curriculum. Its role within the discipline of computer science has greatly diminished over time, if not vanished altogether, and specialists in that area are now to be found mainly within other disciplines, in particular, mathematics and the physical sciences. For example, this trend is discussed in some detail in the insightful and delightfully refreshing memoir of Trefethen [3], *An Applied Mathematician's Apology*—see, in particular, his Sect. 6, pages 15–18; see also Kahan [4]. A central concern of my book is this regrettable, downward trajectory of numerical analysis within computer science and how it can be arrested and suitably reconstituted. Resorting to a biblical metaphor, numerical algorithmics (NAS&E), as envisioned in this monograph, is neither old wine in new bottles, nor new wine in old bottles, but rather this emerging discipline is a *decantation of an age-old vintage* that can hopefully find its proper place within the larger arena of computer science, and at what appears now to be an opportune time.

Acknowledgements

In writing this short monograph, I have been greatly inspired by *Number: The Language of Science* by Tobias Dantzig [5] and *Algorithmics: The Spirit of Computing* by David Harel and Yishai Feldman [6]. These two classics have lent their titles to Chaps. 2 and 3 of this book. And my writing has also been closely guided by *An Introduction to Mathematics* by Alfred North Whitehead [7], a beautiful and today sadly-forgotten masterpiece that was written to address, first and foremost, the philosophy of the subject. Indeed, the focus of my book is also on the underlying "philosophy" of numerical computation rather than on the technical details of particular classes of numerical algorithms and their convergence, complexity, and implementation.

In addition to thanking my mentors to whom this book is dedicated and whose algorithmic genius has always been a source of inspiration, it is a pleasure also to thank Anne Greenbaum, Randy LeVeque, Nick Trefethen, Tom Trogdon, and Eugene Zak for their helpful comments on portions or all of this book's manuscript or its earlier incarnation (Nazareth [8]). Of course this feedback does not imply that they have endorsed the proposals herein or are implicated in shortcomings and errors in my book, for which I bear sole responsibility. I am also very grateful to my incisive and always-gracious editor, Wayne Wheeler, and the efficient production staff at Springer. And lastly, and therefore first and foremost, I thank my wife, Abigail Reeder Nazareth, for her wise counsel from the perspective of the "other culture" (arts and humanities). Without her love, friendship, and joie de vivre, the many hours spent at the keyboard writing the manuscript would have been an exercise devoid of meaning.

Bainbridge Island, WA, USA
September 2022

John Lawrence Nazareth
larrynaz@uw.edu

References

1. Nazareth, J.L.: The Newton-Cauchy Framework: A Unified Approach to Unconstrained Nonlinear Minimization. Lecture Notes in Computer Science 769, Springer, Berlin (1994)
2. Nazareth, J.L.: DLP and Extensions: An Optimization Model and Decision Support System. Springer, Heidelberg (2001)
3. Trefethen, L.N.: An Applied Mathematician's Apology. SIAM, Philadelphia (2022)
4. Kahan, W.: The Numerical Analyst as Computer Science Curmudgeon. https://people.eecs.berkeley.edu/~wkahan/Curmudge.pdf (2002)
5. Dantzig, T.: Number: The Language of Science, 4th edn. Free Press, Macmillan, New York (1954)
6. Harel, D., Feldman, Y.: Algorithmics: The Spirit of Computing, 3rd edn. Springer, Berlin (2012)
7. Whitehead, A.N.: An Introduction to Mathematics. Henry Holt and Company, New York. Reprinted by Forgotten Books, 2010. www.forgottenbooks.org (1911)
8. Nazareth, J.L.: Numerical Algorithmic Science and Engineering within Computer Science: Rationale, Foundations, and Organization, 29p. http://arxiv.org/abs/1903.08647 (2019)

Contents

Chapter 1
The Big Picture: Mathematics, Science and Engineering

1.1 Introduction

Algorithms that operate on numbers and embody the spirit of scientific computing are the primary focus of this book. In subsequent chapters, we will discuss its two undergirding concepts, namely, *number* and *algorithm*, and the *numerical disciplines* that result when these two fundamental concepts are combined.

However, before we embark on that discussion, it will be useful to consider the broader context within which our subject matter resides, i.e., the encompassing disciplines of mathematics, science, and engineering. This will enable us to clarify the nomenclature associated with these three broad arenas of human endeavor and thereby set the stage for the subsequent chapters of this book.

1.2 Arenas and Their Interfaces

A picture being worth a thousand words, let us premise our discussion on the iconic image shown in Fig. 1.1. The three labeled bands in this figure identify the aforementioned *arenas* of mathematics, science, and engineering, and each will now be considered in turn.

Mathematics, the core arena, is classically partitioned into *algebra* (including foundations of mathematics and the development of number systems), *geometry*, and *analysis*. A beautiful introduction to this broad classification can be found in *The Princeton Companion to Mathematics*, edited by Gowers et al. [1]; see, in particular, its description of different modes of mathematical thinking: "algebra versus geometry" and "algebra versus analysis." An earlier and also comprehensive overview is the three-volume survey, *Fundamentals of Mathematics*, of Behnke et al. [2].

Within the integrated discipline, "pure" mathematics is symbolized by the inner perimeter of the mathematics arena of Fig. 1.1, and "applied" mathematics by its outer

J. L. Nazareth, *Concise Guide to Numerical Algorithmics*,
SpringerBriefs in Computer Science,
https://doi.org/10.1007/978-3-031-21762-3_1

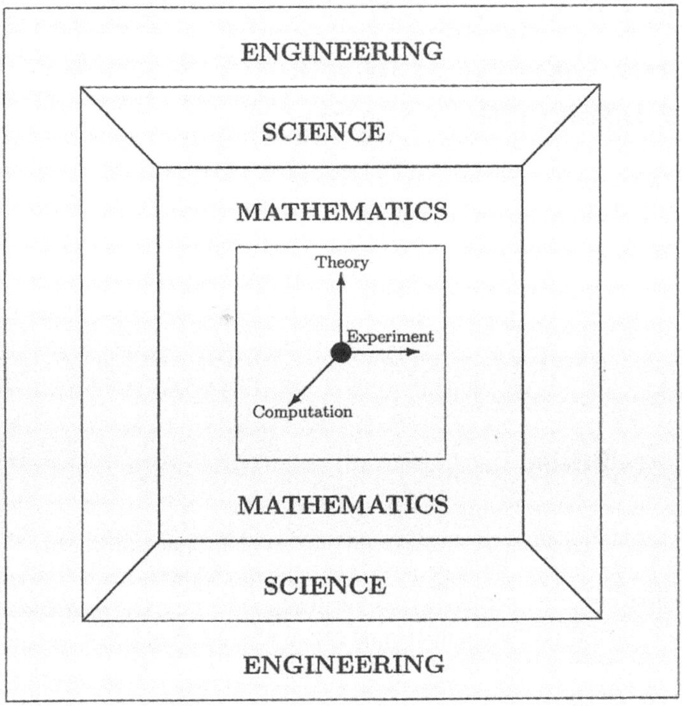

Fig. 1.1 Iconic depiction of relationships between disciplines

perimeter, bordering the science and engineering arenas. However, when making a distinction between pure and applied mathematics, it is worth taking into consideration the views of Hardy [3], one of Britain's most eminent mathematicians, as expressed in his classic summing up of his life's work, *A Mathematician's Apology*. For Hardy, there is indeed a sharp distinction between pure and applied mathematics, but he asserts that this has very little to do with *practical utility*. In his view, both facets of the subject involve the creation of very precise and logically-coherent symbolical systems. But, for pure mathematicians, this is an end in itself. In contrast, applied mathematicians seek to fit their symbolic constructs to physical reality, although their mathematical creations often remain purely theoretical and unverified, and are sometimes even unverifiable by observation or experiment. Thus, both pure and applied mathematicians are fully capable of creating what Hardy calls "real" mathematics. He contrasts this with "school," or "dull," mathematics, which he asserts has *everything to do with its utilization for practical purposes.* It would perhaps have been more charitable to use the word "applicable,", or "utilitarian," but Hardy was not one to mince words; indeed, he states explicitly with regard to his own mathematical contributions: "I have never done anything useful."

Hardy further asserts that what distinguishes real mathematics from school, or applicable, mathematics is that results in the former case are often "deep" and have wide-ranging implications. The two examples he cites date back to the Greek era, namely, the discoveries that there is *no greatest* prime number and that the square root of the number 2 is *irrational*. (Both can be proved very simply, and Hardy supplies perhaps the clearest proofs in all the vast mathematical literature.) In contrast, applicable mathematics may be subtle, even elegant, and sometimes its theorems require difficult and exceedingly complicated proofs. But they are not deep; for example, the proofs that a particular optimization algorithm converges globally to a desired solution or has a local, superlinear rate of convergence. Although Hardy's manifesto is well worth reading in its entirety, these issues will not be pursued here. We will retain the "pure" vis-à-vis "applied" distinction within the arena of mathematics as it is commonly understood, our approach being more in accord with views expressed by the great philosopher and mathematician, Whitehead [4], in *An Introduction to Mathematics*. And for another fascinating perspective on this topic, see the memoir of Trefethen [5], *An Applied Mathematician's Apology*.

Surrounding mathematics is the arena of science, often partitioned into the physical, chemical, and biological sciences. Further partitioning would identify the many specific sciences within each of these three broad subdivisions. (Note that here we are considering only the so-called "hard" sciences; in particular, although not exclusively, the natural sciences, which stand in contrast to the so-called "soft" sciences, for example, political science or the social sciences.) The subfields of science that interface with mathematics and to which the word "mathematical" is prefixed, can be viewed as occupying the inner perimeter of the science arena. Thus in our schema, the terms "mathematical science" and "applied mathematics" are overlapping designations, the former reflecting the perspective of science and the latter the perspective of mathematics. For example, the region wherein applied mathematicians and physicists find common ground is called mathematical physics; applied mathematicians and biological scientists intersect in the region called mathematical biology. Note also that "theoretical" and "mathematical" are sometimes considered to be synonymous designators for scientific disciplines, for example, theoretical physics or theoretical chemistry. However, as we shall see later in this chapter, we prefer to reserve the term "theoretical" for a particular *modus operandi* within each of the three arenas.

The engineering arena also has many subdivisions: mechanical, chemical, electrical, and so on. In this case, the inner perimeter symbolizes the interface with science, specifically the subject known as "engineering science," and the outer perimeter represents "applied" engineering in its usual sense, i.e., the engineering of utilitarian objects premised on science and mathematics, for example, bridges, airplanes, and digital computers. The added diagonal lines at the corners of the science arena, which explicitly link the inner and outer arenas, serve as a reminder that engineering is also connected to mathematics. From the perspective of the engineer, the linking diagonals represent "mathematical engineering"; from the perspective of the mathematician, they represent the applicable region known as "engineering mathematics." These diagonal lines also add an appealing visual dimension to the figure. When one focuses one's gaze on it for a short period of time, these added lines enliven the image so that it shifts, back-and-forth, between a pyramid and a well. From the first perspective, mathematics lies at the apex of a pyramid, flowing downward to science and engineering. From the alternative perspective, the mathematics arena lies deep within a well, beneath science and engineering, and derives its motivation and thrust from these other two arenas.

1.3 Modi Operandi

The three axes at the center of Fig. 1.1 depict the three main *modes*, or forms of investigation, that are employed within *every* branch of mathematics, science, and engineering, namely, the *theoretical*, *experimental*, and *computational* modi operandi. They apply to *any* discipline within the arenas of Fig. 1.1. (The central dot, from which the three axes emanate, represents any such discipline.) Thus evolutionary biology, for example, can be investigated in theory, by experiment in the laboratory, or computationally via simulations on a computer.

Notice that "theoretical" does not necessarily imply the use of mathematics; for example, much of evolutionary biology theory is non-mathematical. And "computational" is relevant across the board. In particular, the term "computational computer science" is *not* redundant, because, for example, the properties of hashed symbol tables could be studied either theoretically or computationally (via simulation on a computer). Note also that the terms "computational science" or "computational science and engineering" are sometimes used to identify a *discipline* that is a counterpart to computer science and engineering. However, this creates unnecessary confusion and it is preferable to reserve the term "computational" for the third *modus operandi*.

Because the computer can be used as a laboratory for performing experiments, the distinction between the "experimental" and the "computational" modes can sometimes become blurred; see, in particular, *Mathematics by Experiment*, the landmark monograph of Borwein and Bailey [6]. The term "empirical" could then be used to designate the union of these two modes, the counterpart to "theoretical," and it can be symbolized by the *plane* defined by the two horizontal axes of Fig. 1.1.

1.4 Summary

We have called the three-arena schema in Fig. 1.1 an "icon," because it is akin more to a "compound symbol" for the complex interrelationships between mathematics, science, and engineering than a strict pictorial representation of them.

The inner perimeter of each arena—mathematics, science, and engineering—represents the "pure" side of its associated subject, and the outer perimeter represents the "applied" side. Mathematics "applied" borders science (and engineering) "pure"; science "applied" borders engineering "pure." And every subfield within each of the arenas, symbolized by the central dot, has three main modi operandi that correspond to the three axes emanating from the dot: theory, experiment, and computation.

Certain fields traverse the boundaries between the three arenas and are called interdisciplinary. For example, statistics traverses the boundary between mathematics and science, uniting mathematical probability, or measure theory, on the one hand, and the science of statistical data, on the other. Computer science (CS) originated with the formal models of computation developed by mathematical logicians, almost a decade before the invention of the electronic computer. The subject then evolved over many decades, and in tandem with electronic, digital computer developments, into a separate discipline that unites science and engineering. Because digital computers, both their software and hardware components, are themselves engineered objects, the discipline is often designated today as computer science and engineering (CS&E) or electrical engineering and computer science (EECS).

In subsequent chapters, we consider particular topics—numerical algorithmics, numerical analysis, and scientific computing—and where they fit into the overall schemata of Fig. 1.1. We shall see that the discipline of numerical algorithmics finds its natural home within computer science (CS&E); that the discipline of numerical analysis has been largely repatriated to pure and applied mathematics; and that scientific computing, also known as computational science and engineering, is the modern modus operandi for investigating problems and models that arise within the arenas of science and engineering, and for which the foregoing two numerical disciplines, in conjunction, can provide an effective computing platform.

References

1. Gowers, T., et al.: The Princeton Companion to Mathematics. Princeton University Press, Princeton (2008)
2. Behnke, H., et al.: Fundamentals of Mathematics. Volume I: Foundations of Mathematics/The Real Number System and Algebra. Volume II: Geometry. Volume III: Analysis. The MIT Press, Cambridge (translated by S.H. Gould) (1974)
3. Hardy, G.H.: A Mathematician's Apology. Martino Fine Books, Eastford, Connecticut, 2018 (1940)
4. Whitehead, A.N.: An Introduction to Mathematics. Henry Holt and Company, New York. Reprinted by Forgotten Books, 2010. www.forgottenbooks.org (1911)
5. Trefethen, L.N.: An Applied Mathematician's Apology. SIAM, Philadelphia (2022)
6. Borwein, J., Bailey, D.: Mathematics by Experiment. A.K. Peters, Nantick (2004)

Chapter 2
Number: The Language of Science

2.1 Introduction

Children learn to speak a human language at a very early age. Then, a little later, they will learn to read and write in that spoken language. And, soon afterwards, they will be taught the addition and multiplication tables and decimal arithmetic, ideally without the aid of an electronic calculator. What do all these learned activities have in common? *They all involve the use of symbols.*

It is our ability to operate with symbols—spoken, written, and sometimes even hand-signed—that sets us apart and is the very hallmark of the human species. In a masterful work, *The Symbolic Species,* the eminent anthropologist and neurologist, Terrence Deacon [1] has indeed characterized human beings as such, as has the great humanistic philosopher Ernst Cassirer [2] in his recently-revived study in three volumes, *The Philosophy of Symbolic Forms.* An accessible précis of this magisterial work is *An Essay on Man*, which Cassirer [3] published a year before his death. Let us therefore examine more closely what is meant by the term "symbolism."

2.2 Symbolism in Human Languages

Most people have an intuitive notion of the meaning of the word "symbolic," namely, the use of "something" to represent, signify, and stand for "something else." For example, a weather forecaster on the nightly TV news might employ a little box containing a yellow circle that represents the sun to predict a sunny tomorrow. Alternatively, the circle may be colored yellow with varying intensities in order to indicate the level of predicted sunshine, ranging from bright yellow, when the next day will be hot, to a paler shade, when it is predicted to be merely warm. And the box containing a yellow circle might be used in yet a third way, to depict the *logo* of the Society of Meteorologists to which our certified TV weather forecaster belongs. We see that

J. L Nazareth, *Concise Guide to Numerical Algorithmics*,
SpringerBriefs in Computer Science,
https://doi.org/10.1007/978-3-031-21762-3_2

the colored box is being employed in *three* very different senses, which specialists in linguistics distinguish by the names *iconic*, *indexical*, and *symbolic*, a terminology that was introduced by the philosopher Charles S. Peirce in the 19th Century (see Justus Buchler [4]). He used the term *sign* to embrace all three usages and reserved the name "symbolic" for the third, which lies at the very foundation of modern human language.

Informally stated, a sign is a stimulus pattern, or signal, that has a meaning, and the way that the meaning is attached to the sign tells us whether it serves as an icon, an index, or a symbol. Thus, an icon is a sign that bears a physical *resemblance to* the "something else" it is chosen to represent, as in our first example, where the yellow circle within the box resembles the sun. An index is a sign that *correlates* with the "something else" in our environment that it signifies, as in our second example, where the shade of yellow within the box correlates with the level of sunshine. Finally, a sign, now quite possibly just an arbitrary pattern, is said to be a symbol when it "gets its meaning primarily from its mental association with other symbols and only secondarily from its resemblance or correlation with environmentally relevant properties" (quoted from the excellent lecture notes of Port [5]). We have seen this in our third example, where the yellow box, with a circle within, serves to symbolize the organization of people who qualify as meteorologists.

The "box" in the foregoing example is a *visual* sign. But signs in general can run the gamut from visual to audible to tactile, even to symbols that arise in our dreams. Indeed, any signal, or pattern, that is accessible to our senses can serve as a sign in one or more of its three manifestations. The subject is fraught with subtlety. For example, Bow-wow can be an index. So can Brrr..rr, uttered with varying intensities when we feel cold. The road sign STOP is an icon for a dog, but for us it is a symbol within the context of all the other road conventions, for example, YIELD. In place of the aforementioned box with a yellow circle within it, one could equally well have used the abbreviation 'MS' or the words 'Meteorological Society'. Most words are symbols in this sense. Moreover, there are word-like symbols and non-word symbols (as in "sign" language for humans deprived of speech). The claim made by Deacon [1] and others is that only the human species is capable of full-blown symbolism, in particular, through the various forms of spoken and written human language and its ultimately refined expression that is modern mathematics. This symbolizing ability developed in parallel with human brain development over an extended period of at least a million and a half years. In contrast, Deacon speculates that other species of animals are capable of using only iconic and indexical signs and do most of their thinking on the basis of associated visual, audible, and olfactory images (and perhaps other types too that are not available to humans).

We humans live in a symbolic world and the ability to symbolize is both the source of our greatest strength and simultaneously a source of weakness. We capture the world through a "net" spun from symbolic words—spoken, written, signed, or even just silently comprehended—that provide us with our primary means for locating and obtaining food, attracting mates, and establishing status, the three activities that occupy much of a human being's waking hours. Think for a moment of the Oxford dictionary! Its organization in alphabetical word-order is apparently simple and linear. But observe that each letter of the (Roman) alphabet has meaning only in relation to the other twenty-five. And every alphabetized word in the dictionary is explained in terms of other words. Suppose we took all the dictionary entries, i.e., the words that are explained in the Oxford dictionary, and listed them instead in twenty-six columns on a very large sheet of paper: the words that start with the letter ‘a’ in the first column, the letter ‘b’ in the second, and so on. Let us now go, in turn, through each entry and its corresponding explanation—for example, “*dictionary*: a reference book listing alphabetically terms or names important to a particular subject or activity along with discussion of their meanings and applications”—and on our sheet of paper let us draw straight lines, which can be thought of as pieces of nylon thread, that connect the word currently being explained to each of the different words in its explanation. (In our example, the word ‘dictionary’, in the fourth column, would have twenty-one threads that connect it to the twenty-one different words in its explanation.) Repeat this procedure for all the words on the sheet of paper. The resulting, unbelievably-dense network of nylon threads, knotted together at each dictionary word, can be imagined as the “symbolic net” by means of which we English-speakers “fish” out the meaning of our daily world! And the same holds true for the multitude of other human spoken and written languages.

2.3 From Words to Numbers

Mathematics is the most precise symbolization of them all. Beginning with the concept of number and its representation by decimal numerals, i.e., sequences composed from the symbols 0, 1, 2, ..., 9, it has evolved over many centuries into the magnificent edifice which today serves as the “language” of modern science.

Nowadays, as noted earlier, most schoolchildren learn *number representation* at an early age, along with the basic arithmetic operations on decimal *numerals*. But the *concept of number* itself is far from elementary, a fact highlighted by the British mathematician Littlewood [6], a distinguished algebraist, in a chapter titled ‘Numbers’ within his classic, *A Skeleton Key of Mathematics* (italics mine):

> A necessary preliminary for any proper understanding of mathematics is to have a clear conception of what is meant by number. When dealing with number most people refer to their own past handling of numbers, and this is, usually, not inconsiderable. Familiarity gives confidence in the handling, but not always an insight into the significance. The technique of manipulating numbers is learned by boys and girls at a very tender age when manipulative skill is fairly easily obtained, and when the understanding is very immature. At a later stage, when the faculty of understanding develops, the technique is already fully acquired, so that it is not necessary to give any thought to numbers. To appreciate the significance of numbers it is necessary to go back and *reconsider the ground* which was covered in childhood. Apart from specialized mathematicians, few people realize that, for example, the number [numeral represented by] 2 can have *half a dozen distinct meanings*. These differences in meaning are reflected in the logical definitions of number.

Our task now is to “reconsider the ground.” But before we proceed to a discussion of Littlewood’s “half a dozen distinct meanings” of a number, let us first take a brief look back into the history of the number concept.

2.4 History and Background

This history is beautifully recounted in *Number: The Language of Science* by Dantzig [7], a landmark book that first appeared in 1930 and then in several subsequent editions (and indeed has lent its title to our present chapter). Albert Einstein himself is said to have endorsed this book as follows (italics mine):

> This is beyond doubt the most interesting book on the *evolution of mathematics* that has ever fallen into my hands. If people know how to treasure the truly good, this book will attain a lasting place in the literature of the world. The evolution of mathematical thought from the earliest times to the latest constructions is presented here with admirable consistency and originality and in a wonderfully lively style.

As Dantzig notes and illustrates with interesting examples, several species of animals and birds, and even some insects, have a rudimentary *number sense*. For example, consider the following characterization of the number sense of humans and other animal species, as stated by the cognitive scientist, Dehaene [8], in his book *Consciousness and the Brain* (italics mine):

> The peculiar way in which we compare numbers thus reveals the original principles used by the brain to represent parameters in the environment such as a number. Unlike the computer it does not rely on a digital code, but on a continuous quantitative internal representation. *The brain is not a logical machine, but an analog device.* Randy Gallistel [a Professor of Psychology and Cognitive Science at Rutgers University, New Jersey, USA] has expressed this conclusion with remarkable simplicity: 'In effect, the nervous system inverts the representational convention whereby numbers are used to represent linear magnitudes. Instead of using number to represent magnitude, the rat [like Homo Sapiens!] uses *magnitude to represent number.*'

In other words, the *rudimentary number sense* of humans is analog in its nature and not significantly different from that of other animals. But *the ability to count*, and, as we shall soon discuss, *the ability also to symbolize number*, appears to be restricted to human beings.

Dantzig tells us that counting with the aid of the digits of our hands, and sometimes both hands and feet, provided primitive man with a very elementary arithmetic and an associated number vocabulary. The most common system was based on the ten digits of our two hands and this is the root of today's decimal system. But there were other number bases that have survived within primitive tribes, even into our modern era; for example, the quinary—base five, utilizing just one hand—which was used by the natives of the New Hebrides; the vigesimal—base twenty, utilizing the digits of both hands and feet—used by the Mayan people of Central America; and even binary—base two, using just our two hands, sans digits—used by a western tribe of the Torres Strait.

Later as human civilizations rose and fell—Babylonian, Egyptian, Greek, Roman, and others—so did their number systems and associated vocabularies for counting. For example, the Babylonians used base sixty, which survives to the present day in the way we count the seconds and minutes of an hour. However, it was only with the discovery of the *positional system* for recording decimal numbers, coupled with the elevation of the symbol "zero" to *full symbolic-number status*, that modern arithmetic was placed on a solid foundation, heralding the birth of mathematics as we know it today.

Dantzig [7] states this beautifully and in an inimitable style as follows (italics are his, except where noted):

> Arithmetic is the foundation of all mathematics, pure or applied. It is the most useful of all sciences, and there is, probably, no other branch of human knowledge which is more widely spread among the masses.
>
> On the other hand, the *theory of numbers* [i.e., integers; and italics mine] is the branch of mathematics which has found the least number of applications. Not only has it so far [namely, at the time of publication of his book or subsequent editions] remained without influence on technical progress, but even in the domain of pure mathematics it has always occupied an isolated position, only loosely connected with the general body of the science.
>
> Those who are inclined towards a utilitarian interpretation of the history of culture would be tempted to conclude that arithmetic preceded the theory of numbers. *But the opposite is true* [italics mine]. The theory of integers is one of the oldest branches of mathematics, while modern arithmetic is scarcely four hundred years old.
>
> This is reflected in the history of the word. The Greek word *arithmos* meant number, and *arithmetica* was the theory of numbers even as late as the seventeenth century. What we call arithmetic today was *logistica* to the Greeks, and in the Middle Ages was called .... *algorism*.

Dantzig tells us that the Greeks were as masterful in "arithmetica," the theory of (whole) numbers, as they were in geometry, and they were the first to introduce mathematical rigor into these subjects. But they lacked a proper symbolism for numbers. Greek mathematicians thought of numbers, namely, integers and fractions, or ratios of integers, in terms of geometric objects. Their mathematics was rooted in Euclidean geometry and other visualizations, for example, blocks of objects arranged in triangles and squares, rather than in arithmetic and algebra. Numbers were viewed as magnitudes, or segments located on a one-dimensional line. For a detailed illustration, see the selections from Euclid's *Elements* in the compilation, *God Created the Integers*, by Hawking [9].

Further illustrations are provided by the exceedingly clever *geometric* arguments that can be used to prove that the square root of the number 2 is an irrational number. (Since these proofs can now be easily found via an internet search, we will not reproduce them here.) They are formulated in a way that *might conceivably* have been discovered by the Pythagoreans themselves, and they stand in marked contrast to the modern algebraic proofs. Another illustration is given in Fig. 2.1, which again demonstrates how the Greeks might conceivably have multiplied two numbers viewed as magnitudes.

A unit magnitude is first established, as shown in the figure, which equals the length BD. Then, by using the lengths $a = OA$, $b = DE$, $c = OF$, and $1 = BD$ defined in the figure and the similarity of triangles, we can demonstrate that c is the product of a and b as follows:

$$a/1 = AG/BG = OG/DG = FG/EG = c/b \text{ and hence } c = ab.$$

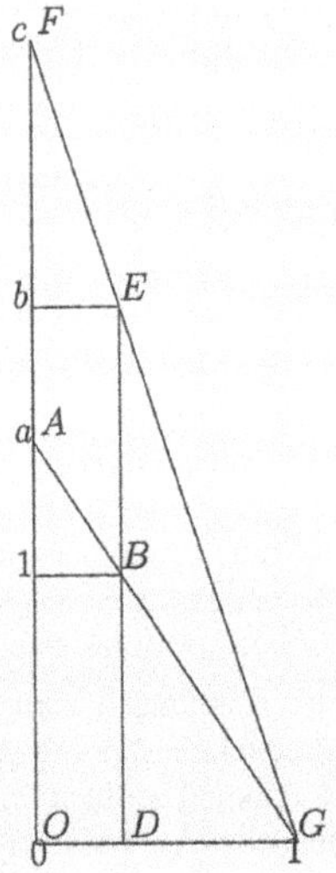

Fig. 2.1 Geometric multiplication

The simple fact is that *lengths, or magnitudes, are not numbers.* They are concrete visualizations, iconic and indexical in the terminology introduced in the previous section, rather than symbolic. In particular, a segment with *no* length does not exist, which is perhaps why the Greeks failed to arrive at a true conception of the number "zero." Likewise, they presumably had no *symbolic* concept of negative numbers, again because a segment of negative length does not make sense either. When it became necessary to identify a number by a written symbol, the Greeks resorted to using letters of their alphabet, for example, the number "ten" was denoted by "ι" and the number "hundred" by "ρ". The subsequent Roman system was hardly an improvement, for example, "ten" being denoted by "X" and "hundred" by "C". Indeed, the symbolic representations used millennia earlier by the Sumerians and the Egyptians, although not positional, were in some ways superior. For details, see again Dantzig [7].

In tracing the evolution of the number concept and its positional, decimal representation, it is useful to consider the mechanical devices that have been invented over the ages to facilitate elementary arithmetic. Early man perhaps used notches on a tree trunk, or collections of pebbles on a beach, for *unary* counting, i.e., premised on base 1, which was very likely the very first number system devised by humans. The counting board and the abacus were invented later, with the latter surviving even into the modern era.

A very basic abacus is depicted in Fig. 2.2, which is reproduced from Dantzig [7], but with annotations added to identify its top and bottom and to number its rungs. Other abaci come in a wide variety of different forms and are available to this day. Babylonians would have required an abacus with sixty beads on each rung instead of ten. And, in marked contrast, the Greeks would have had little use for the beads

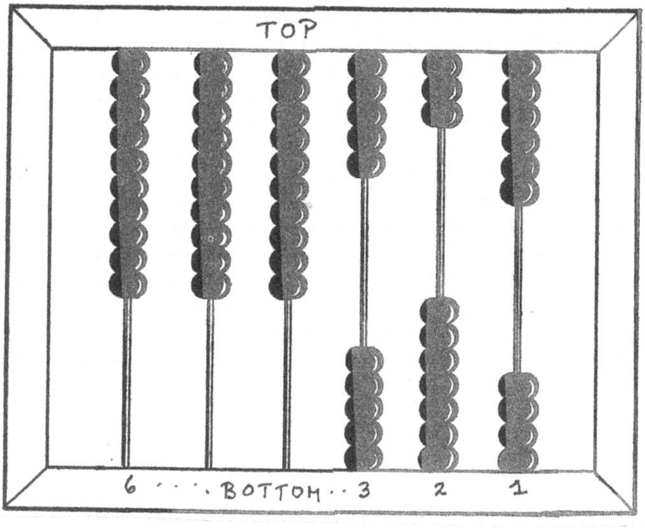

Fig. 2.2 A simple abacus

of the abacus, because in their view numbers corresponded to magnitudes, i.e., to *segments of the rungs* themselves on which the individual beads were hung.

The simple abacus of Fig. 2.2 provides us with a convenient metaphor for tracing the evolution of the number concept. Assume for subsequent discussion that adjacent beads at the top are inactive, and, in the initial state of such an abacus, assume all the beads on the six rungs are placed at the top. Rungs will be identified by the numbers indicated in the figure, i.e., rung 1 is the rightmost rung of the abacus. Now, if an individual were to begin counting on such an abacus, using the primitive, *unary* system—let us call him or her a *unarist*—then beads would simply be moved, one at a time, from the top to the bottom, starting with rung 1, and with the accumulating counts collected in groups of ten. For example, when our unarist reached the count of "ten," then the ten beads on rung 1 would have been moved to the bottom. When the counting had continued to "eleven," then one bead on rung 2 would have been moved to the bottom; when it reached "twenty," then ten beads on each of the first two rungs would have been moved to the bottom, and so on. On the other hand, a so-called *abacist* would count on that device using a positional, decimal system. The counting up to "nine" would be identical to the unarist's. However, when the count reached "ten" the abacist is faced with an ambiguous situation. He/she might mirror the unarist. Or alternatively, one bead on rung 2 might be moved to the bottom and the ten beads on rung 1 moved back to the top. When the counting then increased by one to "eleven," one bead on rung 1 would once again be moved to the bottom. The mechanical counting could then proceed to twelve, thirteen, and so on, and when it reached "twenty" an ambiguity would again arise and could be resolved as indicated above. Eventually the abacus would be in the (unambiguous) state shown in Fig. 2.2 and would indicate that the count had reached the number "five hundred and seventy four." The counting procedure as just envisioned is purely mechanical, no symbolization being involved.

It was the mathematicians of ancient India who made the crucial step of *symbolizing* the foregoing procedure. Ten adjacent beads at the *top or bottom on any rung* were conceptualized as vanishing into an empty column that they called "sunya." *This sunya was thereby elevated to full-fledged number status. Today we call it "zero" and represent it by the symbol "0".* Furthermore, on any rung, one bead at the bottom was given a unique symbol, today we use "1", two adjacent beads at the bottom are symbolized today by "2", and so one up to nine adjacent beads at the bottom symbolized by "9". The mechanical counting procedure on the abacus along with other symbolized arithmetic operations, for example, addition or multiplication, of the decimal system can then be conveniently transferred away from the abacus.

What seemed like a rather simple modification was, in fact, a truly monumental advance—the genius of the modern, symbolic system of decimal notation—which Dantzig [7] describes as follows:

> ...the Indian *sunya* was destined to become the turning-point in a development without which the progress of modern science, industry, or commerce is inconceivable. And the influence of this great discovery was by no means confined to arithmetic. By paving the way to a generalized number concept, it played just as fundamental a role in practically every branch of mathematics. In the history of culture the discovery of zero will always stand out as one of the greatest single achievements of the human race.

Persian mathematicians later adopted this positional number system based on the number "zero," and its embracing Islamic civilization then transmitted it to the West, which is why the symbols even today are called Arabic numerals. Henceforth in our discussion we will refer to them and the associated positional representation of numbers by this latter name, whilst not forgetting the origins of this great idea.

Dantzig [7] tells us that the struggle between the *abacists*, who defended the old tradition, and the *algorists*, who advocated the reform, lasted in the Western tradition from the eleventh to the fifteenth centuries. It was during the period of the Renaissance in the sixteenth century that the algorists achieved final victory and from then on the progress of mathematics was unhampered. And few would argue today with the observation that mathematics in full-flower, both pure and applied, has evolved from that root concept of symbolized number.

2.5 The Symbolism of Mathematics

Once whole numbers *were fully symbolized*, the discipline of mathematics was placed on a solid foundation and a more rapid evolution could begin. In *An Introduction to Mathematics*, a deceptively simple but simultaneously deep and penetrating glimpse into the *philosophy* of the subject, Whitehead [10] highlights this achievement as follows (italics mine):

> For our present purposes, however, the *history* of the notation is a detail. The interesting point to notice is the admirable illustration which this numeral system affords of the importance of a good notation. By relieving the brain of all unnecessary work, a good notation sets it free to concentrate on more advanced problems, and in effect increases the mental power of the race.

And again (italics mine):

> ....by the aid of symbolism, we can make transitions in reasoning almost mechanical by the eye, which otherwise would call into play the higher faculties of the brain.
>
> It is a profoundly erroneous truism, repeated by all copy-books and by eminent people when they are making speeches, that we should cultivate the habit of thinking of what we are doing. *The precise opposite is the case.* Civilization advances by extending the number of important operations which we can perform without thinking. Operations of thought are like cavalry charges in a battle—they are strictly limited in number, they require fresh horses, and must only be made at decisive moments.

Whitehead [10] then proceeds to elaborate on why the symbolization of "zero" was such an important advance and it is well worth quoting him again in full, for his valuable insight, as well as the grace of expression and subtle humor whereby he makes his argument (italics mine except where noted):

> It is interesting to note how important for the development of science a modest-looking symbol can be. It may stand for the emphatic presentation of an idea, often a very subtle idea, and by its existence make it easy to exhibit the relation of this idea to all the complex trains of ideas in which it occurs. For example, take the most modest of all symbols, namely, 0, which stands for the *number* zero [italics his]. The Roman notation for numbers had no symbol for zero, and probably most mathematicians of the ancient world would have been horribly puzzled by the idea of the number zero. For, after all, it is a very subtle idea, not at all obvious. A great deal of discussion on the meaning of the zero of quantity will be found in philosophical works. Zero is not, in real truth, more difficult or subtle an idea than the other cardinal numbers. What do we mean by 1 or by 2, or by 3? But we are familiar with these ideas, though we should most of us be puzzled to give a clear analysis of the simpler ideas which go to form them. The point about zero is that we do not need to use it in the operations of daily life. *No one goes out to buy zero fish.* It is in a way the most civilized of all the cardinals, and its use is only forced on us by the needs of cultivated modes of thought. Many important services are rendered by the symbol 0, which stands for the number zero.

Whitehead then gives three key reasons for celebration of the symbol 0, which we can summarize as follows:

1. The first use of 0 was to make the *Arabic notation* possible—no slight service as he says.
2. It made possible the growth of the modern conception of *algebraic form*—simply stated, the ability to write equations like $ax + by = 0$, where relations between *variables*, i.e., x and y, and constants, or *parameters*, i.e., a and b, on the left-hand side, are equated to the number zero on the right-hand side.
3. Whatever the number x may be, $0 + x = x$, and $0 \times x = 0$. This makes it possible to then *generalize*, i.e., to assimilate particular equations into broader categories of equations. Thus the particular linear equation above is seen to belong to the broad category of general linear equations.

And Whitehead concludes his celebration of the symbolization of the number zero and his account of its implications, as itemized above, for the flowering of mathematics, with the following truly memorable observation (italics mine):

> These three notions, of the *variable*, of *form*, and of *generality*, compose a sort of mathematical trinity which preside over the whole subject. They all really spring from the same root, namely from the abstract nature of the science.

2.6 From Numbers to Number Systems

2.6.1 Positive Numbers

With a clear symbolization of the whole numbers—also called natural numbers or cardinal integers—firmly in place, mathematics could now proceed to the *generalizations* of number, i.e. the "half a dozen different meanings" of the numeral "2" as mentioned earlier in the quotation from Littlewood [6].

Let us briefly trace this progression, beginning with the idea of positive fractions. To continue Whitehead's observation quoted earlier: although no one goes out to the fishmonger to *literally* purchase zero pounds of fish, a household cook would certainly go there to buy, say, a half-pound's worth. In other words, the basic concept of a fraction is obvious and was well-known to the civilizations of the past. The Greeks thought of the concept in terms of *ratios* of whole numbers—hence rational numbers, or "rationals"—which they represented in iconic or indexical terms as ratios of magnitudes, or lengths. From this geometric-based viewpoint, the Pythagoreans then made the great discovery that there existed lengths that could *not* be expressed as the ratio of whole numbers, for example, the length of the hypotenuse of a right-angled triangle whose other two sides are of unit length, which today we denote as $\sqrt{2}$. They deemed such numbers to be incommensurable ratios, leading to the category that we continue today to call "irrational" numbers.

These three categories of number, namely, integral numbers, fractional numbers, and incommensurable, or irrational, numbers can be put together into a *single class of numbers*, which today we call "*real numbers*." (Note that so far we have considered only positive numbers and the number 0.)

How do we represent this collection of real numbers? Let us return again to the perspective of the Greeks and represent them as indexical segments on a line as shown in Fig. 2.3, which is taken from Whitehead [10].

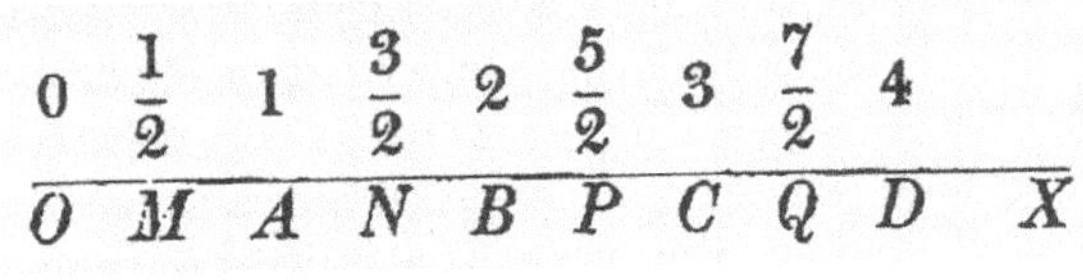

Fig. 2.3 Symbolic and indexical representation of numbers

It requires that a unit length be established as depicted by the length OA and then all other numbers assume their natural length along the infinite line that extends to the right, a few evenly-spaced integers and fractions being shown explicitly in symbolic form, each associated with an alphabetic letter. A natural ordering of the numbers is established by this linear depiction.

An alternative, symbolical way to represent real numbers is to return to the decimal place-value system, or Arabic notation, for representing whole numbers, which as noted earlier was firmly established following the triumph of the algorists. The idea of its extension to represent *fractions* was soon afterwards discovered by several mathematicians, most notably in 1585 by Simon Stevin, a Flemish mathematician and engineer. For whole numbers, the place value is determined by powers of 10 and for fractions, the place-value system could be extended by using powers of 1/10, i.e., using tenths, hundredths, thousandths, and so on, to the right of a decimal point. Thus, for example, the fraction 1/2 would be represented as 0.5, i.e., five-tenths, or 2 1/4 represented by 2.25, i.e., two plus two-tenths plus five-hundredths.

Without going into a detailed justification here, we can note that any fraction on the line can be represented symbolically by either a *terminating* place-value decimal or by an *infinite* sequence of digits after the decimal point that repeats periodically. For example, 1/3 by 0.33333.... repeated indefinitely or 1/7 by 0.142857... and with that sequence of digits repeated indefinitely.

Irrational numbers, on the other hand, correspond to infinite sequences of digits with no discernible pattern. An irrational number can always be approximated by a rational number, and to an arbitrary degree of accuracy, by truncating its symbolic representation, thereby retaining only a finite number of digits. And given this fact, Littlewood [6] explains in masterful fashion the *mathematical* necessity for real numbers as follows:

> It is pertinent to enquire why it is necessary to introduce real numbers since these constitute so vast an extension of the rationals, apparently to so little effect, since to every real number, one can obtain a rational approximation to any degree of accuracy. The necessity for the real numbers is illustrated by an important class of theorems called the *existence theorems*. A query often arises, does there exist a number with such and such a property? With rationals the answer is often "no", whereas with real numbers the answer would be "yes". To make sure that a number will always be existent and ready when it is required, the vast extension of rationals to reals is necessary.

For the simplest illustration of the foregoing, consider the problem of finding a solution to the equation $x^2 - 2 = 0$. If we were to restrict ourselves to the rational numbers, then a solution to this equation does not exist. To solve an equation even as simple as this one, we need the reals.

A few key assertions regarding rationals and irrationals depicted in Fig. 2.3 can now be stated:

1. Between any two *rational* numbers on this line, no matter how close, another *rational* number can be found.
2. Between any two *rational* numbers on the line an *irrational* number can be found.
3. Between any two *irrational* numbers on the line a *rational* number can be found.

4. Fascinating issues related to counting arise from these observations, namely, that the rational numbers are countable, i.e., they can be placed in a 1-to-1 correspondence with the positive integers. On the other hand the real numbers, or in particular, the irrational numbers are not countable. Stated informally, there are "many more" irrational numbers than rational numbers. These ideas are due to Georg Cantor and, in Whitehead's memorable words on the need for the reals: "they are of the utmost importance in the philosophy of mathematical ideas. We are here in fact touching on the fringe of the great problems of the meaning of continuity and of infinity."

2.6.2 Negative Numbers

Finally, the introduction of negative numbers marked the completion of the real number system. Nowadays negative numbers are so commonplace that it is hard to imagine a time when they were controversial. But when one thinks in iconic or indexical terms of magnitudes, or lengths, or indeed of actual objects, for example, beads on an abacus, then negative numbers are indeed difficult to conceive. However, when one begins to view them from a symbolic standpoint, i.e., as members of a symbolic system, they make complete sense.

Once "zero" is accepted as a full-fledged number, the simplest way to introduce negative numbers is as follows: given any (positive) real number, which we symbolize by x, then the defining property of its negative, which today we symbolize by $-x$, is that when one adds it to x one obtains zero. And if x is restricted to just the whole numbers (cardinal integers) or to just the positive rational numbers, it is obvious that the same argument applies, leading to definitions of negative integers and negative rationals, respectively.

There are alternative ways of arriving at negative real numbers. Instead of considering the real numbers (positive and including zero) of Fig. 2.3 in themselves, if one considers the *operations* of adding or subtracting them, one can again arrive at the concept of negative numbers, an approach discussed, in detail, for instance in Whitehead [10]. Another mathematically more formal way to introduce *signed* real numbers is via the model of *pairs* of the (positive) real numbers depicted in Fig. 2.3, along with appropriate definitions of equality and the arithmetic operations between such pairs. This is the approach taken, for instance, by Littlewood [6] to which we refer the interested reader for a clear exposition.

One can then complete the symbolic and indexical representation of Fig. 2.3 by extending the real line to infinity in both directions, with negative numbers then being depicted to the left of "zero" and positive numbers to the right. Starting from any given number depicted on this line, other numbers increase progressively when one moves to the right along the line and they decrease progressively when one moves to the left.

In summary, we have collected the positive reals, negative reals, and the number "zero," into the set of *real numbers*, which is traditionally denoted by R. It contains the collection of positive rationals, negative rationals and "zero," called the set of *rational numbers* and traditionally denoted by *Q*. And *R* and *Q* in turn contain the collection of positive integers, negative integers and "zero," which is called the set of *integers* and is traditionally denoted by *Z*. Needless to say, *R*, *Q*, and *Z* contain the whole numbers, or cardinal integers, which we could denote by *W*. These distinct sets *W*, *Z*, *Q*, and *R* collectively highlight the assertion of Littlewood [6], quoted at the very outset of our discussion of number and which we can now recall again in conclusion, namely, that few other than specialists in mathematics are fully appreciative of the fact that the "number 2 can have half a dozen distinct [mathematical] meanings."

2.6.3 Other Number Systems and Beyond

We can now summarize the present-day view of numbers, which the *Princeton Companion to Mathematics* of Gowers et al. [11] states as follows (italics theirs):

> The modern view of numbers is that they are best regarded not individually but as parts of larger wholes called *number systems*; the distinguishing features of number systems are the arithmetic operations—such as addition, multiplication, subtraction, division, and extraction of square roots—that can be performed on them.

This viewpoint has led mathematicians to a variety of other number systems, for instance, the following:

1. The Complex Numbers: we saw earlier that a solution (also called a root) of a polynomial equation as simple as $x^2 - 2 = 0$ motivates the creation of the real number system. Likewise, finding a solution to an equally simple polynomial equation $x^2 + 1 = 0$ necessitates the creation of a new symbolic number $i = \sqrt{-1}$ and then the system of complex numbers of the form $a + bi$, where a and b are real numbers. This new system is normally represented by *C* and it obviously contains all the previously introduced systems, namely, *W*, *Z*, *Q*, and *R*. This also leads to the "fundamental theorem of algebra," namely, that any given polynomial equation with real coefficients has a root in *C*.
2. The Algebraic and Transcendental Numbers: Consider the set of numbers that are solutions, or roots, of the class of polynomial equations with *integer*, or equivalently rational, coefficients. Such numbers, obviously a subset of *C*, are called algebraic. Numbers in *C* that are not algebraic are called transcendental. Interestingly enough, the algebraic numbers are countable and the transcendental numbers are not.
3. The Infinitesimal Numbers: Consider any given positive, real number, $x > 0$. It is clear that there always exists a positive and large-enough integer n such that $1/n$ is less than x. Can we define a number system that contains all real numbers and, in addition, has non-zero elements that a) are smaller than $1/n$, for any given positive integer n, and b) obey arithmetic laws similar to those of the reals? This was answered in the affirmative by the famed mathematician, Abraham Robinson, through his introduction of "hyperreal" numbers and settled

a question that plagued mathematicians for centuries. (Infinitesimals are useful, for example, for conveniently defining the derivative of a function.)

These are but three examples and there are others; see, for example, "Quaternions, Octonions, and Normed Division Algebras" in Gowers et al. [11].

It is almost a truism to state that a true sense of the beauty of mathematics comes from an exposure to number systems in all their depth and subtlety, a subject that the Greeks called logistica, the Middle Ages called algorism, and today is termed modern arithmetic. (Recall again the distinction between logistica and number theory, or the theory of positive integers, which was paradoxically called arithmetica by the Greeks.) As Gowers et al. [11] tell us in their *Princeton Companion to Mathematics*: "..... a true appreciation of the real number system depends on an understanding of mathematical analysis, ..." And again: "This view of numbers [as number systems] is very fruitful and provides a springboard to abstract algebra."

The underlying *structure* of the foregoing basic number systems was subsequently extended, generalized, or relaxed, leading to many other key mathematical concepts, for example, groups, rings, and fields, vector spaces, matrix and tensor algebra, functional analysis, complex analysis, and so on, thereby evolving, over time, into the highly-elaborated mathematics of today, a subject that is masterfully surveyed in Gowers et al. [11]. When we use the phrase "rubric of number" in subsequent chapters, we mean this overarching umbrella of modern-day mathematics.

References

1. Deacon, T.W.: The Symbolic Species: The Co-Evolution of Language and the Brain. W.W. Norton & Company, New York (1997)
2. Cassirer, E.: The Philosophy of Symbolic Forms. Volume 1: Language. Volume 2: Mythical Thinking. Volume 3: Phenomenology and Cognition, Routledge. (Translated from the German by S.G. Lofts and reviewed by Adam Kirsch, "The Symbolic Animal," in The New York Review of Books, April 8, 2021, pp. 51–53) (1923–1929)
3. Cassirer, E.: An Essay on Man: An Introduction to a Philosophy of Human Culture. Yale University Press, New Haven (1944)
4. Buchler, J.: The Philosophical Writings of Peirce, selected and edited by the author and with an Introduction. Dover Publications, New York (1955)
5. Port, R.F.: Lecture Notes on Linguistics, L103, Indiana University, September, 2000. www.cs.indiana.edu/~port/teach/103/sign.symbol.html (2000)
6. Littlewood, D.E.: The Skeleton Key of Mathematics: A Simple Account of Complex Algebraic Theories. Dover, New York (republication of the original 1949 edition) (2002)
7. Dantzig, T.: Number: The Language of Science, 4th edn. Free Press, Macmillan, New York (1954)
8. Dehaene, S.: Consciousness and the Brain. Viking, The Penguin Group, New York (2014)
9. Hawking, S. (ed.): God Created the Integers. Running Press, Philadelphia (2005)
10. Whitehead, A.N.: An Introduction to Mathematics. Henry Holt and Company, New York. Reprinted by Forgotten Books, 2010. www.forgottenbooks.org (1911)
11. Gowers, T., et al.: The Princeton Companion to Mathematics. Princeton University Press, Princeton (2008)

Chapter 3
Algorithmics: The Spirit of Computing

3.1 Introduction: What is an Algorithm?

Stated informally, it is a finitely-terminating, teleological, or goal-seeking, dynamical process that may be defined *conceptually* as a symbolical object, or realized *concretely* in the form of computer software, or perhaps even discovered *empirically* within nature. Although now inextricably linked with the electronic computer, the idea of an algorithm can be traced back to antiquity. Classical algorithms include, for example, Euclid's for finding the highest common factor of two positive integers (third century, B.C.), Euler's for finding a cycle that traverses all edges of an undirected network, Gaussian elimination for solving a system of linear equations, and Newton's for finding the root, or solution, of a nonlinear equation. And the word "algorithm" itself is derived from the name of the great ninth century (A.D.) Persian mathematician and scholar, Al-Khowarizm.

The popular science writer, Berlinski [1], characterizes a *symbol-based algorithm* in the following poetic manner:

> **In the logician's voice:**
>
> an algorithm is
>
> a finite procedure,
>
> written in a fixed symbolic vocabulary,
>
> governed by precise instructions,
>
> moving in discrete steps, 1,2,3, ...,
>
> whose execution requires no insight, cleverness,
>
> intuition, intelligence, or perspicuity,
>
> and that sooner or later comes to an end.

J. L Nazareth, *Concise Guide to Numerical Algorithmics*,
SpringerBriefs in Computer Science,
https://doi.org/10.1007/978-3-031-21762-3_3

Similarly, the renowned computer scientist and one of the founders of the field, Knuth [2], has described the basic idea underlying symbol-based computing as follows (italics mine):

> An *algorithm* is a precisely-defined sequence of *rules* telling how to produce specified output information from given input information in a finite number of steps. A particular representation of an algorithm [in a particular computer language] is called a [computer] *program* ....
>
> .....computing machines (and algorithms) do not compute only with *numbers*. They deal with information of any kind, once it is represented in a precise way. We used to say that a sequence of symbols, such as a name, is represented inside a computer as if it were a number; but it is really more correct to say that a number is represented inside a computer as a *sequence of symbols*.

In current public discourse, a "recipe" in a cookbook is often used as an analogue for "algorithm." But, in reality, recipe (say within a soup-cookbook) stands in relation to algorithm in much the same way that numeral, along lines discussed in the previous chapter, stands in relation to number. Like number, the concept of "algorithm" is far from elementary. Because, rather than being *a single recipe*, the analogue of an algorithm is, in fact, closer to an *entire chapter* of the soup-cookbook, wherein different choices of ingredients (inputs to an algorithm) lead, via a sequence of procedural steps, to different soups (outputs of an algorithm).

Note, in particular, that a symbol-based algorithm must always come to a halt and produce its output after a *finite* number of steps. If this is not the case, for example, if on some particular input, its procedural steps enter an infinite loop, then we will use the term *program*. In other words, a program—itself perhaps a slightly closer analogue to "recipe"—is not required to produce an answer for each and every given input. (Another frequently used term in this setting is "*computer* program," the concrete realization of an algorithm or program as a finite list of instructions in a computer programming language.) We see that every algorithm is a program within its prescribed model of computation, but every program is *not* necessarily an algorithm. These terminological distinctions may seem pedantic, but as we shall see later in this chapter, they point to one of the most fundamental issues in the theory of computation, the so-called "halting problem."

3.2 Theoretical Foundations: The Grand Unified Theory of Computation

It was only relatively recently that the concept of a *general algorithm* was given its *formal* definition. This axiomatic description of computation, in the 1930s, by a group of distinguished mathematical logicians—Kurt Godel, Alonzo Church, Stephen Kleene, A.A. Markov, Emil Post, and, above all, Alan Turing—has been likened in importance to the axiomatization of geometry by Euclid. It provides the theoretical foundation for the discipline of computer science—more on that subject later in this essay—and it is viewed as one of the great intellectual achievements of the twentieth century. Seemingly different formulations of an "algorithm" were shown to be to be equivalent, leading to what became known later, within the new discipline of computer science, as the Church-Turing thesis, or, more descriptively, as the *"grand unified theory of computation."* This all-embracing characterization is due to Moore and Mertens [3], who state it as follows:

> In 1936, computer science had its own grand unification. In the early twentieth century, driven by the desire to create a firm underpinning for mathematics, logicians and mathematicians invented various notions of an "effective calculation" or "mechanical procedure"—what we would call a program or algorithm today. Each of their definitions took a very different attitude towards what it is meant to compute. One of them defines functions recursively in terms of simpler ones; another unfolds the definition of a function by manipulating strings of symbols, and, most famously, the Turing machine reads, writes, and changes the data in its memory by following a set of simple instructions.
>
> Turing, Kleene, Church, Post, and others showed that each of these models can simulate any of the others. What one can do, they all can do. This universal notion of computation, and the fact that it transcends what *programming language* we use, or what technology we possess, is the topic ....[under consideration].

Moore and Mertens [3] then proceed to describe "the three great models of computation proposed in the early twentieth century—partial recursive functions, the lambda-calculus, and Turing machines—and show they are equivalent to each other."

Likewise, in a truly masterful work, Harel and Feldman [4] describe this great achievement more colorfully as follows (boldface theirs):

> Ever since the early 1930s researchers have suggested models for the all-powerful absolute, or ***universal***, computer. The intention was to try to capture that slippery and elusive notion of "effective computability," namely the ability to compute mechanically. Long before the first digital computers were invented, Turing suggested his primitive machines and Church devised a simple mathematical formalism of functions called the ***lambda calculus*** ...[the basis of functional programming languages]. At about the same time Emil Post defined a certain kind of symbol-manipulating ***production system***, and Stephen Kleene [a student of Church] defined a class of objects called ***recursive functions***. ..... All these people tried, and succeeded, in using their models to solve many algorithmic problems for which there were known "effectively executable" algorithms. Other people have since proposed numerous different models for the absolute, universal algorithmic device. Some of these models are more akin to real computers, having the abstract equivalent of storage and arithmetic units, and the ability to manipulate data using control structures such as loops and subroutines, and some are purely mathematical in nature, defining classes of functions that are realizable in a step-by-step fashion.
>
> The crucial fact about these models is that they have *all* been proven equivalent in terms of the class of algorithmic problems they can solve. And this fact is still true today, even for the most powerful models conceived.
>
> That so many people, working with such a diversity of tools and concepts, have essentially captured the very same notion is evidence of the profundity of that notion. That they were all after the same intuitive concept and ended up with a different-looking, but equivalent, definition is justification for equating that intuitive notion with the results of those precise definitions. Hence the CT [i.e., Church-Turing] thesis.

And finally, for a popular rendition of the Church-Turing thesis, which also includes many extraneous personal and historical details, see Berlinski [1], in particular, his Chaps. 6, 8, 9, and 10.

3.3 A Hierarchy of Theoretical Models

Here we will not attempt a comprehensive survey. Instead, our purpose is to present a *carefully-selected set* of models of computation in *a novel, reverse-chronological* order, which progressively drills down to the essence of a symbol-based algorithm and a universal, or general-purpose, computer. We will thereby establish a *hierarchy of models* that progresses from the realistic to the highly abstract.

We begin with Donald Knuth's MMIX realistic computational model, which embodies a very basic programming language and a machine on which it runs. Next, numerous details that are extraneous from a conceptual standpoint can be discarded, leading to a much simpler computational model called a register, or random-access, machine and stored program (RAM and RASP). When additional, and again conceptually unneeded, details are stripped-off, one obtains even simpler computational models known as Turing-Post programs (TPPs) and universal TPPs. And further refinement then leads us to the most fundamental expression of the Church-Turing thesis, namely, Turing machines (TMs) and universal TMs. The equivalence of the foregoing models of computation and a related and fundamental issue known as the "halting problem" will then conclude this discussion.

3.3.1 Knuth's Realistic Model: The MMIX Computer

The great computer science pioneer, Donald Knuth, created a realistic model of computation based on a low-level and (hopefully) long-lived computer language, together with a conceptual machine on which programs written in this language could be run. This is described in detail in a fascicle, Knuth [5], which he wrote in support of his monumental book series, beginning with Knuth [6]—a classic of computer science—to which subsequent volumes were added over the years.

Knuth's rationale for not relying on one of the computer languages available at the time was that they go in and out of fashion, as stated in his own words as follows:

> ....what language would that be? In the 1960s I would probably have chosen Algol W; in the 1970s, I would have had to rewrite.....using Pascal; In the 1980s, I would surely have changed everything to C; in the 1990, I would have had to switch to C^{++} and then to Java. In the 2000s, yet another language would no doubt be *de rigueur* [and in the 2010s that language may well have been F$^{\#}$ or Python].

Instead, Donald Knuth designed his language to be "powerful enough to allow brief programs to be written for most algorithms, yet simple enough so that its operations are easily learned." It runs on a hypothetical computer MMIX that is "very much like every general-purpose computer designed since 1985, except that it is perhaps nicer." Let us now briefly describe this language and computer and then extract the essential aspects in order to define what can be termed Knuth's realistic model of computation.

The MMIX machine's symbolic vocabulary is based on binary digits. It has 2^{64} cells (8-bit bytes) of addressable *memory* and 2^8 general-purpose *registers*, each capable of holding an octabyte (8 bytes, or 64 bits). In addition, there are 2^5 special-purpose, octabyte registers. Data is transferred from the memory to the machine's registers, transformed in the registers by other instructions, and transferred back to memory from the registers.

The machine uses the so-called RISC, or reduced-instruction, architecture with 256 different *operation codes*, or commands. Instructions in MMIX have only a few formats:

1. OP X, Y, Z;
2. OP X, YZ; or
3. OP XYZ;

where OP denotes the operation code, and the remaining quantities denote upto three operands. These operands identify registers of the machine holding data for the instruction and sometimes specify data for direct use within the instruction, i.e., X, Y, and Z identify registers, and YZ and XYZ denote operands that are used directly. The *set of instructions* covers loading and sorting, arithmetic operations, conditional operations, bitwise and bytewise operations, floating-point operations, jumps and branches, and so on. Additionally, *input/output* primitives permit the transfer of data between input or output files and memory (via special registers). Furthermore, Knuth [5] extended this MMIX language to a low-level, assembly language he called MMIXAL that allowed alphabetic names to stand for numbers and a label field to associate names with memory locations and registers.

The MMIX language is transparent to its underlying machine and resides at the *opposite* end of the spectrum from the high-level programming languages mentioned in the foregoing quotation, which shield the user from the computer on which they are implemented and can rapidly become out of date. *However, a detailed description of MMIX is not needed here.* What matters is that the machine possesses certain key components: a memory, a suitable repertoire of instructions, and a mechanism for input of data and output of computational results.

MMIX serves as a powerful and *realistic* model of computation and a means for expressing algorithmic ideas in a precise way. In this setting, *an algorithm takes the form of a legitimate MMIX program*, which is executed in a linear stream under the control of a *location counter*. The location counter identifies the program instruction to be executed, the "current" instruction. If this is a branch, or jump, instruction, its execution causes the location counter to be updated so that it points to the *chosen* instruction of the program. Otherwise, after execution of the current instruction, the location counter is incremented by 1, in order to identify the next instruction to be executed in the linear sequence.

An MMIX program and its associated location counter, the embodiment of an algorithm, are assumed so far to be executed by an unspecified "outside agency." A key idea underlying general-purpose computation is that *MMIX instructions can themselves be held in memory*, and modified within it, if desired. Each instruction is defined to be 32 bits (4 bytes) long, where the first of these four 8-bit bytes defines the operation code—hence the fact that the language has $2^8 = 256$ choices—and the remaining three bytes define (upto three) operands, the aforementioned quantities X, Y, Z, YZ, and XYZ. (Again, the details do not concern us here, but we can observe and appreciate the extreme elegance of Knuth's design.) A "fixed *hardwired* unit" incorporates the location counter, the hardware for executing floating-point and other instructions, additional registers, the machine "clock," and so on. This so-called central processing unit, or CPU, of the machine corresponds to the "outside agency" mentioned above. It fetches a programmed algorithm's instructions from where they are stored in memory and identified there by means of the location counter as described earlier, and decodes and executes them in a linear stream (unless a branch is encountered). This is the standard *fetch-execute* cycle of a modern, general-purpose, or *universal*, computer.

MMIX provides an excellent means for teaching introductory computer programming and opening a window into the more advanced computer languages mentioned above. However, we will not employ it further in this book. It is the *existence* of MMIX as *a realistic model for machine computation*, along with the fact that MMIX captures the key distinction between an "algorithm" and a "universal computer," that is central to our present discussion. This "algorithm versus universal computer" distinction, an underlying theme of the present section, will repeat itself within each major computational model discussed below.

3.3.2 Register, or Random-Access, Computational Models

Random-access machines (RAMs) and random-access stored programs (RASP) are *idealizations*, or abstractions, of realistic models of computation such as MMIX. The essence of this abstraction involves the following:

1. Simplifying the addressable memory and registers of MMIX and the input/output mechanism while simultaneously removing restrictions on register size, or capacity.
2. Greatly reducing the instruction set.
3. Making explicit the distinction between "algorithm" and "universal computer."

The resulting random access machine, or RAM, is summarized in Fig. 3.1.

Its main components consist of an addressable *memory*, a read-only *input tape* with associated read head, a write-only *output tape* with associated write head, and a *program* with an associated location counter, or more accurately, location *pointer*.

The memory of a RAM is an unbounded set of cells, or "words," numbered 1, 2, 3, ..., which define their addresses. Each cell can hold a positive or negative

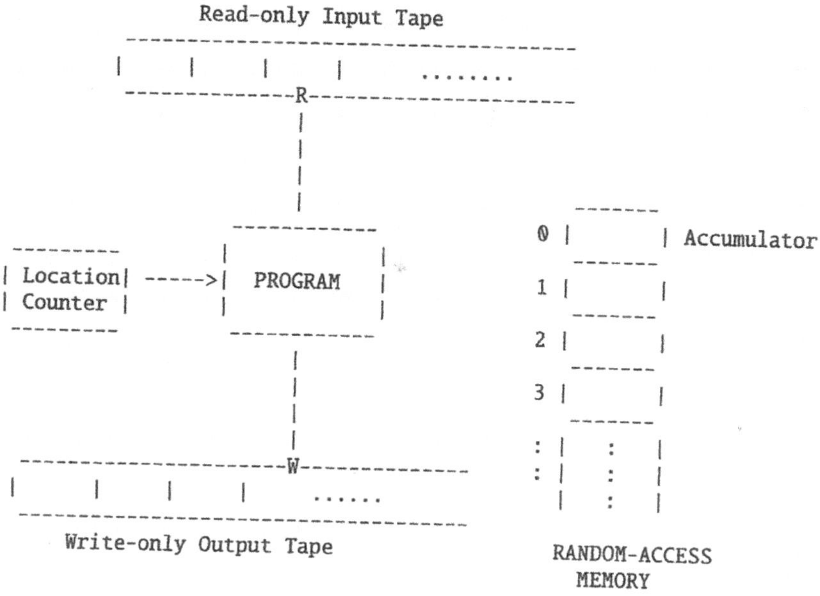

Fig. 3.1 Random access machine (RAM)

integer or the number zero, defined by a binary pattern of 0s and 1s, and of arbitrary size. The relatively large set of registers in Knuth's MMIX model, where they are distinguished from memory cells, are now condensed in the RAM model into a single register, called the *accumulator*. It too can hold an arbitrary integer, or bit pattern, and all computation takes place within this accumulator, which corresponds to address 0 of the memory. *Cells with addresses 1,2, 3, ..., are also called machine registers of the RAM,* hence the alternative name—"register machine"—for this computational model, i.e., the accumulator is simply the first cell, or register, of the addressable memory. It is distinguished from them in terms of its function, as will be described in more detail below. Henceforth, the content of memory cell, or register, i will be represented by $c(i)$ for $i = 0, 1, 2, \ldots$.

Computation in a RAM is determined by a *program*, which is *not* stored in memory and cannot modify itself. This program consists of a sequence of (optionally *labeled*) *instructions* that are defined by the *operation codes* and *operands* in the following tabulation:

Operation code	Address
LOAD	operand
STORE	operand
ADD	operand
SUB	operand

(continued)

(continued)

Operation code	Address
MULT	operand
DIV	operand
READ	operand
WRITE	operand
JMP	label
JGTZ	label
JZERO	label
STOP	

Observe that these instructions fall into five main groups: load/store between the accumulator and memory cells; arithmetic operations between integers of arbitrary size and where the DIV operation uses the ceiling function to ensure the result is an integer; read/write between input/output tapes and accumulator; unconditional or conditional jumps to a labeled instruction of the program; and, finally, the instruction to stop.

Each instruction consists of two fields noted above—an "operation code" and an address field containing an "operand"—and there are three choices for the latter:

1. An integer, say i, directly specified;
2. The contents of the cell, or register, of memory with an address defined by i, i.e., the quantity $c(i)$, or
3. The contents of the word of memory addressed by *one level of indirection* using the specified integer i, i.e., the quantity $c(c(i))$—this third option within a RAM is necessary in order to allow addresses to vary dynamically within a computation. Without this option, all addresses within a program would be predetermined integers and they could not be chosen at the time of execution, for example, by reading them from the input tape.

The foregoing three options are determined by the way that the operand is specified in the address field of the instruction, namely, $=i$, or i, or $*i$, respectively. For example, the program instruction that performs multiplication is defined as follows:

1. MULT $=i$ means $c(0) \leftarrow c(0) \times i$;
2. MULT i means $c(0) \leftarrow c(0) \times c(i)$;
3. MULT $*i$ means $c(0) \leftarrow c(0) \times c(c(i))$.

Other arithmetic operations are defined in a similar way.

Consider again the instruction that loads information from memory into the accumulator:

1. LOAD $= i$ means $c(0) \leftarrow i$;
2. LOAD i means $c(0) \leftarrow c(i)$;
3. LOAD $*i$ means $c(0) \leftarrow c(c(i))$.

The STORE instruction is defined analogously with the left-arrow reversed; but note that STORE = *i* is meaningless.

The input tape is a sequence of cells, each of which can hold an arbitrary bit pattern, or integer. It has a read head that identifies the cell to be read into the memory or accumulator by a READ instruction. Thus, for example, 'READ *i*' means that the bit pattern, or integer, under the read head is transferred to the cell with address *i*, which must be nonnegative. (If $i = 0$ then it is transferred to the accumulator.) After its execution, the read head is always moved one cell to the right. Analogous comments hold for the output tape and its corresponding WRITE instruction.

Finally, 'JMP *L*' indicates an unconditional jump to the instruction with label *L*. (Recall that instructions can be optionally labeled.) Substituting JGTZ and JZERO for JMP changes the instruction to a conditional jump governed by $c(0) > 0$ and $c(0) = 0$, respectively.

The execution of a program is governed by the location counter, which points to the current instruction to be carried out by the RAM. If this is a jump instruction then the location counter may be set to point to the instruction determined by the corresponding label. For example, 'JGTZ *L*' will set the location counter to the program instruction labeled *L* when the integer in the accumulator is positive. Otherwise, it is incremented by 1. On all non-jump instructions, the location counter is incremented by 1, i.e., the next instruction in the program sequence is pointed to for execution by the machine. Execution ceases when a STOP instruction is encountered or when an instruction is invalid, for example, 'MULT **i*' with $c(i) < 0$.

We highlight the following characteristics of a RAM:

- The instruction set corresponds to a small subset of the instructions in MMIX. (Note also that the DIV operation uses the ceiling function to ensure the result is an integer.) This RAM instruction set could be augmented with other MMIX-type instructions as desired without any significant alteration of the RAM's computational capability, in principle. Put another way, the instruction set of MMIX can be simulated by RAM programs, or subroutines, written using its basic instruction set.
- All computation within a RAM takes place within the single accumulator. Additional accumulator registers could be added to the model to enhance efficiency, but again they would not alter the basic computational power of the model.
- In contrast to MMIX, memory cells and the accumulator of a RAM have unbounded capacity. Furthermore, no limit is placed on the number of memory cells in a RAM.
- A RAM does not store its programs in memory or modify it. As such, it models an *algorithm* rather than a *general-purpose computer*, a distinction that we have already noted within the earlier MMIX model.
- We have also noted the need for indirect addressing in order to allow addresses to vary dynamically within a computation.
- A RAM could easily be extended to (an equivalent) *rational arithmetic machine* where data consists of rational numbers, or ratios of integers, represented implicitly by holding the numerator and denominator in memory.

A random access stored program, or RASP, machine is identical in memory design and instruction set to a RAM and, in addition, employs an encoding scheme to translate each instruction into a bit sequence that can be stored in memory. Each instruction uses two memory cells: the first holds the operation code of the instruction encoded as an integer, and the second holds the operand. The encoding of each operation has two options, indicating whether the associated operand is to be used directly or as an address, i.e., $=i$ or i. The third option of indirect addressing within a RAM, namely, $*i$, is no longer needed, because an instruction in memory can now be modified at run, or execution, time. In other words, a RASP machine can *simulate* the RAM operation of indirect addressing. We need not be concerned here with further details of the encoding scheme.

Analogously to a RAM, the location counter points to the first of the two registers holding the current instruction. After it is executed, the location counter is incremented by 2 for all non-jump instructions. The operand in a jump instruction now specifies the register to which the location counter is reset, for example, JMP i or JGTZ i. (Note that the choice of operand $= i$ is meaningless.) The RASP machine executes a program stored in memory under the control of a "hardwired program," or central processing unit (CPU), analogously to the situation discussed earlier for the MMIX machine. Again, a key point to note is that *a RASP machine is a model of a general-purpose stored program, or universal, computer.*

Further detail on the RAM and RASP models, if desired, can be found, for example, in Aho et al. [7], although regrettably this reference does not emphasize the foregoing "algorithm versus universal machine" distinction.

3.3.3 The Computational Models of Turing and Post

The models of computation of Alan Turing and Emil Post were formulated in the 1930s, well before the advent of the electronic, digital computer. Although Turing-Post and Turing models preceded MMIX and RAM/RASP in the historical development of computing, it is convenient to view them through the lens of these more recent models, i.e., as *idealized* machines that are obtainable by *further abstraction* of a random-access, or register, model. Turing-Post and Turing models have the simplest structure of them all, yet they do not sacrifice basic computational power, i.e., they retain the ability to compute, albeit much less efficiently, the same class of functions as the RAM and RASP models, the so-called *partial recursive functions* mentioned in a foregoing quotation.

In the approaches of both Turing and Post, the random-access memory of a RAM or RASP, along with its input and output tapes as depicted in Fig. 3.1, are condensed into a *single* tape that is infinite in one direction, say downward, and divided into individual memory cells. *Usually this tape is depicted horizontally in diagrams,* but in order to emphasize its conceptualization of the memory of a RAM, we find it more convenient now to depict it vertically in Figs. 3.2 and 3.3.

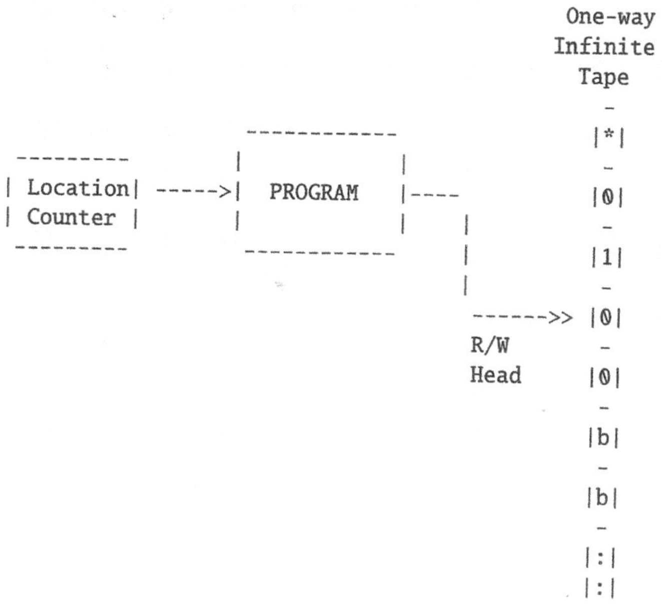

Fig. 3.2 Turing-Post machine

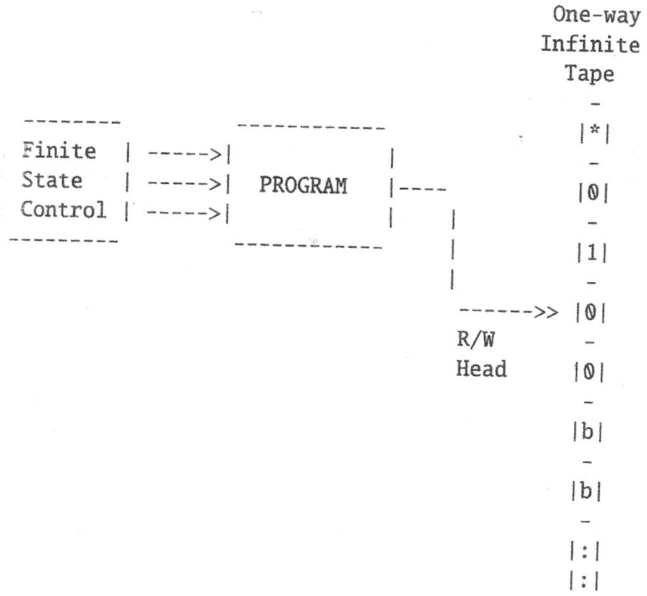

Fig. 3.3 Turing machine

Instead of an arbitrary integer, or bit pattern, a cell on this tape can store only a single binary digit, i.e., the symbols '0' or '1', or it is left unwritten, or blank, denoted by the symbol 'b'. In addition, the uppermost cell is identified by the symbol '*'. (These four symbols comprise the alphabet of the computational model.) One particular cell on this tape is scanned by a *tape head*, which can *read* or *write* to this cell and then move to the *adjacent* cell immediately above or below, or remain stationary. In contrast to a RAM, the luxury of randomly-addressable memory cells, each of which has unbounded capacity, is no longer available. Furthermore, as we shall see, the instruction set of a RAM is further simplified within a Turing-type model.

3.3.3.1 Turing-Post Programs (TPPs) and Universal TPPs

The Turing-Post program model of computation is depicted in Fig. 3.2. It is premised on the original formulation of Emil Post, which was closer in *spirit* to the modern digital computer than Turing's approach, but it derived its impetus from the fundamental *analysis* of Turing. The RAM location counter and program of Fig. 3.1 are retained, but this program now consists of instructions of an even simpler variety as show in Table 3.1.

In Table 3.1, β has four choices for the WRITE and IF instructions, making for a total of eleven instructions within the table. A Turing-Post program is an (optionally) labeled sequence of instructions from this table. As in a RAM, they are executed in a linear sequence with the current instruction being identified by the location counter. Following execution, the location counter is incremented by 1 unless a branch is encountered. *In this approach to computability, an algorithm can again be viewed as just such a Turing-Post program that terminates on all inputs.*

Analogously to the transition from a RAM to a RASP machine, a universal TPP machine is obtained by using an encoding scheme for instructions and program labels that enables a Turing-Post program itself to be stored on the tape of the machine. Four bits are needed in order to encode an operation code (not all 2^4 patterns are needed) and the label within an IF instruction, or position in a program, can be encoded in a *unary* representation. A *fixed* Turing-Post program can then be devised that is capable of emulating the action of any other TPP, when the former is furnished on its tape with the encoded version of the latter, together with its input data. This fixed

Table 3.1 Turing-post instruction set with β = 0, 1, b or *

Instruction	Meaning
WRITE β	Write the symbol β in the current cell (under the head)
DOWN	Move head down by one cell
UP	Move head up by one cell
IF β GOTO L	Go to instruction labeled L if the current cell is β
STOP	Terminate execution

Turing-Post program defines the associated *universal TPP machine.* Again, we can view it as the equivalent of a "hardwired CPU" of a general-purpose computer.

Further details of the encodings mentioned above are not needed here. An excellent and much more detailed account can be found in Davis and Weyuker [8] and a very accessible account can also be found in Stewart [9]—see his Chap. 19.

3.3.3.2 Turing Machines (TMs) and Universal TMs

A Turing machine is depicted in Fig. 3.3 and it shares many features of a TPP. However, the location counter of a TPP, which points to the current instruction to be executed, is replaced by a "composite pointer" called a *finite state control.* This can assume a *finite* number of states, which can be viewed as positions in a "primitive program" that consists of *quintuples,* each of which is of the following form:

$$(q, \beta, \beta', q', s)$$

- q is a state from the set of states that the finite-state control can assume.
- β is taken from the alphabet $\{0, 1, \text{b}, *\}$ as in the Turing-Post case.
- β' is also a member of the alphabet $\{0, 1, \text{b}, *\}$.
- q' is a member of the set of states.
- s is a member of the set $\{-1, +1, 0\}$.

The set of quintuples can be specified *in any order* and each is *a primitive program line* that is executed by the Turing machine as follows: when the finite state control is in state q and the symbol in the current cell under the R/W head is β then overwrite the current cell with the symbol β', change the TM's control state to q', and move the R/W head one cell up if $s = -1$, one cell down if $s = +1$, and leave it in the same position if $s = 0$. The exception to this rule is when the tape head is already at the uppermost cell and $s = -1$, in which case the tape head stays in the same place. The machine is initially provided with a tape with the uppermost cell containing the symbol *, a finite string of 0s and 1s representing the input, and the rest of the tape containing blanks, i.e., the symbol b. The R/W head is over the uppermost symbol, and the state of the machine is set to a (special) starting state, say, q_s.

The machine looks through the program lines until it finds the quintuple $(q, \beta, ., ., .)$ for which q corresponds to the current state of the machine and β corresponds to the symbol currently under the head. It then executes the program line as described above. If it enters a (special) halting state, say, q_h, or if no quintuple matches the current condition of the machine, then it stops.

There are many variants on the foregoing TM formulation:

- a tape that is *infinite in both directions*;
- a TM with several tapes and corresponding tape heads;
- a tape head that *must move* up or down at each executed step, i.e., s is a member of the set $\{-1, +1\}$;

- a smaller or larger vocabulary of symbols;
- primitive program lines that are quadruples rather than quintuples;
- a *nondeterministic* TM which can *simultaneously execute* a finite number of different outcomes, i.e., its execution sequence is represented by a branching "tree" of outcomes rather than a simple path.

These variants (and others) do not alter the inherent power of the resulting machines—they all compute the same class of (partial recursive) functions within the context (and vocabulary) of the aforementioned "grand unified theory," albeit with increased or diminished efficiency. When efficiency is *not* at issue, perhaps the most surprising of these equivalences is the fact that a nondeterministic TM can be emulated by a deterministic. However, when efficiency of execution comes into the picture, this leads to one of the great open conundrums of computer science, namely, the so-called "(deterministic) polynomial vis-à-vis non-deterministic-polynomial" problem, or "P = NP?" For a detailed discussion of the TM model and its variants, see, for example, Aho et al. [7], Gary and Johnson [10], or Nielsen and Chuang [11].

Finally, we come to the key notion of a Universal Turing Machine (UTM), an idealized model of computation proposed by Alan Turing. It conceptualizes the modern, general-purpose electronic digital computer, but predates, by a decade, the invention of the latter by Presper Eckert and John Mauchly. The idea is much the same as we have seen for earlier models, namely, encode the quintuples, or program lines, of the TM so that they can be represented digitally on the tape, or machine's memory. Then define a *fixed* TM that can simulate any other when furnished with the TM's encoding and input data. This is the desired *universal Turing machine.* The details of this formulation are challenging, of course, and a very readable account of such a UTM can be found in Penrose [12].

3.3.4 Computational Equivalence and the Halting Problem

Let us return now to the issues raised when we began this discussion, namely, the "grand unified theory of computation" and associated questions regarding terminology.

Among the different approaches to computation just described, Alan Turing's proved to be preeminent as *a foundation for the emerging discipline of computer science.* Turing machines compute the class of functions that are termed *partial recursive*, as do almost all the other models described in this essay. The exception is MMIX, which paradoxically is the least powerful of our models, in principle, because its memory is finite, but the most realistic and usable in a more practical sense. MMIX can be idealized to allow memory cells and registers to hold binary integers of arbitrarily large size and to make available an unbounded number of memory cells. This idealized version could then be shown to be equivalent in computational capability to the register (random-access), Turing-Post, and Turing models.

As we have already noted, the computational equivalence of different models and the resulting universal definition of computation within the field of computer science is known as the *Church-Turing Thesis*, which Moore and Mertens [3] characterize as being:

> ....the philosophical stance that has structured computer science since 1936. The *Church-Turing Thesis* states that Turing computability, in any of its equivalent forms, is the right definition of computability—that it captures anything that could reasonably be called a procedure, or computation, or an algorithm. The universal Turing machine is capable of simulating, not just any Turing machine, but any computing device that can be finitely described, where each step accesses and modifies a finite amount of information.

Associated with these results is a second fundamental breakthrough of Turing, which is known in computer science circles as the *halting problem*. (It has profound consequences for the foundations of mathematics and, in particular, it has ties to the work of Kurt Godel that are also detailed in the foregoing reference.) We will describe it informally here and this discussion requires further clarification of our terminology.

We have noted that any Turing *machine*, or any of the other models of computation introduced previously, has an associated *program* that defines its behavior. (For purposes of present discussion, we will use the terms "machine" and its defining "program" interchangeably.) The program is initiated with a specific input furnished on the Turing machine's tape and upon execution it may or may not return a result, i.e., on some particular input the machine may never come to a halt. If the program, or equivalently the Turing machine, halts and produces a result for *each and every* possible input with which it can be supplied then the program will be called an *algorithm*. In other words, *every algorithm is a program, but not every program is an algorithm.*

Let us now ask the following seemingly innocent question: within a chosen model of computation, in particular the Turing model, does there exist a particular *algorithm* that can examine any *program* whatsoever that is defined within the model and determine whether or not that *program* is itself an *algorithm?* This has become known as the *halting problem,* because a variant of this question is as follows: for a chosen model of computation, does there exist a particular and so-called *halting algorithm* which is capable of examining any given program within that model, along with any input for that program, and determine whether or not that program will *halt* on that given input? If the answer to the second form of the question is false, i.e., that a halting algorithm does *not* exist, then obviously so is the answer to the first form of the question.

Note that the algorithm being sought in the foregoing two forms of the question is required to always return a yes/no answer, i.e., if we were to substitute "halting program" for "halting algorithm" in the foregoing questions then the *universal machine* associated with the computational model under consideration would do the job! And indeed, it is by resorting to this universal machine that we can provide a definitive answer to whether or not the desired halting algorithm exists. Recall that the universal machine, or *general-purpose computer*, for the computational model is able to simulate *any other machine* operating on its given input, within that model of computation. We have seen that the universal machine goes about its business by being furnished, in suitably encoded form, with a description of the other machine that is to be simulated, along with the input to the latter. When "other" in the two preceding questions happens to be the universal machine itself, or a suitably contrived variant, i.e., when "a serpent feeds on its own tail," so to speak, then fascinating things can happen. Indeed this how the foregoing question regarding the existence or not of a halting algorithm within the model of computation is resolved!

The first approach is to use an argument based on what is termed *explicit* diagonalization, which is described in a very complete and readable manner by Penrose [12]. The other is a delightfully simple and elegant *implicit* diagonalization argument, which can be found, for example, in Stewart [9]. Both forms of the argument and their far-reaching implications are nicely described in Moore and Mertens [3] to which we refer the reader for further details on the proof. Here let us content ourselves by simply stating the answer to the question raised above: the sought-for halting algorithm does *not exist* and the halting problem is therefore said to be *undecidable.* Put another way, if we were to assume that a halting algorithm within the chosen model of computation did exist then we would be able to obtain a contradiction by constructing a particular program on which our assumed halting algorithm fails.

Note that so far our focus has been on foundational issues regarding the conceptual equivalence of our models of computation and with no regard whatsoever to practicality or to efficiency. Mathematicians known as logicians have had their say and provided the conceptual foundations for the discipline of computer science. We must now turn to other considerations which are also at the heart of the discipline, first to *numerical computation in practice*, and then, albeit only very briefly, to the efficiency, or *computational complexity*, of algorithms.

3.4 Practical Foundations: Floating-Point Model

With the advent of the electronic, digital computer in the 1940s it became necessary to go beyond the theoretical conceptions of an algorithm developed during the previous decade and address issues of practicality, in particular, the limitations of digital computer memory.

In the idealized RAM model discussed previously, recall that each register can hold an integer of arbitrary size, or each pair of adjacent registers can hold a rational number that is arbitrarily large or small. We must now begin to consider how to store and perform operations on the real numbers described in Chap. 2, i.e., the number system that includes integers, rational numbers, and irrational numbers, and that have limits on their range and accuracy when represented in the computer's memory. And we must move beyond the basic arithmetic operations described for the RAM and consider basic arithmetic operations on these represented numbers, which again may not yield results that can be exactly represented. These considerations led to the creation of the finite-precision, floating-point model of computation, which we now set out to describe.

3.4.1 Finite-Precision Representation: Decimal Base

Computer arithmetic is most commonly based on the binary (base-2) and hexadecimal (base 16) number systems. However, because the decimal number system (base 10) is the most familiar, let us explain the main ideas in this system and then summarize the results for an arbitrary base.

The representation of a real number, say *x,* usually requires an infinite number of decimal digits, say, $d_1, d_2, d_3, \ldots$. We will now make the convention that the leading digit is nonzero and with the (decimal) point at the left and say that the number is *normalized*. The true position of the decimal point for *x* is then provided by means of a signed integer, say e, called the *exponent*, which yields a decimal representation of *x* as follows:

$$x = (\pm.d_1d_2d_3\ldots)10^e$$

where $1 \le d_1 \le 9, 0 \le d_j \le 9, j = 2, 3, \ldots$. We observe immediately that

$$|x| \ge (0.1)10^e.$$

In a digital computer, only a finite number of digits, say *t* digits, can be stored. And furthermore, the range of e is restricted to

$$-m \le e \le M$$

where *m* and *M* are positive integers.

If the trailing digits $d_{t+1}, d_{t+2}, \ldots$ are dropped in the above exact representation of *x* then we say the resulting number, say x_c, is obtained by *chopping x*. In this case the error $|x - x_c|$ is bounded by

$$|x - x_c| \le (\text{one unit in the last place})10^e.$$

Therefore

$$|x - x_c| \le \left(10^{-t}\right)10^e.$$

Rounding a number *x* is more common and we will only consider it henceforth. When *x* is rounded to *fl(x)* by adding 5 to digit t + *1* and then chopping, the error is

$$|fl(x) - x| \le (\text{half unit in the last place})10^e.$$

Thus

$$|fl(x) - x| \le 1/2\left(10^{-t}\right)10^e.$$

Note that when x is chopped, the digits d_1, d_2, d_3, …, d_t and the integer e remain unchanged. However, if it is rounded, all these quantities can change. This is why, in subsequent discussion on representable numbers, we change notation to italicized d_j and *e*.

Thus a *representable* floating-point number is, in general, defined as

$$x = (\pm.d_1 d_2 \ldots d_t)10^e$$

i.e., by a *signed t*-digit normalized *mantissa,* or *significant,* $\pm\, d_1 d_2 \ldots d_t$ and an *exponent e* that again satisfies

$$-m \leq e \leq M.$$

Numbers with exponents outside this range are said to spill. At the lower end of the range we say *underflow* and at the upper end we say *overflow.* The number zero is represented as $(.00\ldots0)10^{-m}$.

For any non-zero number x let us now define the *relative error* by

$$\mu = (fl(x) - x)/x.$$

Then, using earlier upper and lower bounds on the above quantities, it is easy to establish that

$$|\mu| \leq 1/2\left(10^{1-t}\right).$$

3.4.2 Finite-Precision Representation: Arbitrary Base

For an arbitrary base, say β, the foregoing results can be extended in a straightforward manner by replacing 10 by β.

Thus

$$x = (\pm.d_1 d_2 d_3 \ldots)\beta^e$$

where $1 \leq d_1 \leq \beta - 1, 0 \leq d_j \leq \beta - 1, j = 2, 3, \ldots$ and

$$-m \leq e \leq M$$

where m and M are positive integers.

And, after rounding, its corresponding *represented* floating-point number *fl(x)* is as follows:

$$fl(x) = (\pm.d_1 d_2 \ldots d_t)\beta^e$$

where $1 \leq d_1 \leq \beta - 1, 0 \leq d_j \leq \beta - 1, j = 2, 3, \ldots$ and again

$$-m \leq e \leq M$$

where m and M are positive integers.

Analogously to the decimal development, we have

$$|x| \geq (\beta^{-1})\beta^e.$$

$$|fl(x) - x| \leq 1/2(\beta^{-t})\beta^e.$$

For any non-zero number x, the *relative error* is defined as before, namely,

$$\mu = (fl(x) - x)/x.$$

Then using earlier upper and lower bounds on the above quantities, it is again straightforward to establish that

$$|\mu| \leq 1/2(\beta^{1-t}).$$

Reorganizing these expressions, we obtain

$$fl(x) = x(1 + \mu) \quad \text{where } |\mu| \leq 1/2(\beta^{1-t}).$$

We see that a *small relative change* in any number x is needed to *represent it exactly*. The quantity μ will *vary* with x, but its upper bound will always be the same number $1/2(\beta^{1-t})$ which henceforth we will call the unit of roundoff error, or *ulp*.

In particular, for the binary base $\beta = 2$, we have

$$fl(x) = x(1 + \mu) \quad \text{where } |\mu| \leq 2^{-t}.$$

3.4.3 Axiomatic Floating-Point Arithmetic and an FP-RAM

Let us now consider the basic arithmetic operations between finite-precision, floating point-numbers that are analogous to the arithmetic operations ADD, SUB, MULT, and DIV between integers on a RAM defined by Fig. 3.1.

Let x and y be *representable* floating-point numbers, so that without having to resort to rounding, we have $x = fl(x)$ and $y = fl(y)$, and let $+$, $-$, *, and / represent the basic arithmetic operations of addition, subtraction, multiplication, and division between x and y. Let # stand for any of these four arithmetic operations.

An idealized, or axiomatized, implementation of floating-point arithmetic would form *fl*(*x* # *y*) as the representable number that is nearest to the *exact* result (*x* # *y*), i.e., *fl* (*x* # *y*) would be the result of rounding the quantity (*x* # *y*) obtained if exact arithmetic were used. It then follows directly from the results obtained in the previous section that

$$fl(x\#y) = (x\#y)(1+\mu) \quad \text{where } |\mu| \le 1/2\left(\beta^{1-t}\right).$$

Note that μ will vary depending upon the operation # and the operands *x* and *y*, but the *bound* on $|\mu|$ is, in each case, the same number (ulp).

It is now a straightforward matter to design a practical FP-RAM machine along the foregoing lines. A register of an FP-RAM will hold a finite amount of information, namely, it can store integers with a finite number of digits or a floating-point number defined by a mantissa with a finite number of digits and an exponent with explicit bounds. The exception is the accumulator, i.e., register 0, which is, say, twice the size of a register, thus permitting the axiomatized arithmetic described above to be performed. The number of registers, or memory cells, can be allowed to be unbounded or alternatively also restricted. Further detail is not needed here, but we will return briefly to this topic in Chaps. 5 and 6.

3.5 Algorithmics

In an invaluable collection of articles discussing the philosophy of computer science, Knuth [2], one of the founding fathers of this discipline, makes the following observation in his subsequent reflections on the subject (italics mine):

> My favorite way to describe computer science is to say that it is the study of algorithms...... Perhaps the most significant discovery generated by the advent of computers will turn out to be that algorithms, as *objects of study,* are extraordinarily rich in interesting properties; and, furthermore, that an algorithmic point of view is a useful way to organize information in general. G.E. Forsythe has observed that "the question: 'What can be automated?' is one of the most inspiring philosophical and practical questions of contemporary civilization.

Indeed, during the early days, there was debate as to whether this new discipline should be called *Algorithmics*—see again Knuth [2], who, in turn, attributes the name to Traub [13]. No other book captures the essential nature of computer science, when viewed from this foundational perspective, than the masterpiece of Harel and Feldman [4], *Algorithmics: The Spirit of Computing*. (Our present chapter derives its title from this classic.) However, what is also very evident from even a quick perusal of Harel and Feldman [4]—a feature we wish to emphasize here, and one that is further highlighted by perusing other popular computer science textbooks, for example, *Algorithms*, by Dasgupta et al. [14] and *Introduction to Algorithms*, by Cormen et al. [15]—is the downgraded role of *numerical computation* within the discipline of computer science. How this deficiency can be rectified is the main topic of this extended essay and its next three chapters.

But to conclude, we touch very briefly on topics that are central to the computer science of today, namely, the efficiency, or computational complexity, of symbol-based algorithms and newer models of computation at the current research frontier.

3.6 Computational Complexity

As computer science evolved into a separate discipline, issues of efficiency, or complexity, of computation came to the fore. As noted by Gowers et al. [16] in *The Princeton Companion to Mathematics* (italics mine):

> Broadly speaking, theoretical computer science [of today] is concerned with efficiency of computation, meaning the amounts of various resources, such as time and computer memory, needed to perform given computational tasks. There are mathematical models of computation that allow one to study questions about computational efficiency in great generality without having to worry about precise details of how algorithms are implemented. Thus, theoretical computer science is a genuine branch of pure mathematics: *in theory, one can be an excellent theoretical computer scientist and be unable to program a computer*. However, it has many notable applications as well, especially in cryptography.

The modern theory of computational, or algorithmic, complexity was spearheaded by Turing Award winners, Juris Hartmanis and Richard Stearns, Stephen Cook and Richard M. Karp, and it identified problem categories such as P (polynomial-time), NP (non-deterministic polynomial-time), NP-complete (the most challenging sub-category of NP problems), NP-hard, P-space, and so on, culminating in one of the great and currently unresolved conundrums of computer science, namely, the so-called "(deterministic) polynomial vis-à-vis non-deterministic-polynomial," or "P = NP?" problem. For an early overview, see Garey and Johnson [10] and for more recent surveys, see, for example, Moore and Mertens [3] and Harel and Feldman [4].

3.7 Algorithmic Systems and Beyond

In our previous Chap. 2, we traced the evolution from the initial symbolization of number to the concept of number systems, and then beyond to modern-day mathematics. Likewise, the conceptualization of a symbol-based algorithm discussed in the present chapter has evolved to a broadened conception of algorithmic systems and beyond to modern-day computer science. Let us briefly itemize some of their underlying models of computation, along with sample references where more detail can be found:

- Cellular automata models developed by Stephen Wolfram [17], including universal versions, which provide the foundation for his proposed "new approach to science" based on such models.

- Analog computing models: see, for example, the "continuous time" model of Moore [18] and its cited antecedents, which are in the tradition of the general-purpose analog computer of Shannon [19]; see also the "magnitude-based, continuous-discrete" CD-RAM model proposed by Nazareth [20], which can potentially be implemented using Hewlett-Packard memristors, as described in Nazareth [21].
- Randomized models—see, for example, Chap. 10 of Moore and Mertens [3]—and, more generally, the quantum models of computation and the universal quantum computer of Deutsch [22]; see, for example, Chap. 15 of Moore and Mertens [3] or Nielsen and Chuang [11] for overviews of this subject.
- Biological-based, associative models of computation (see Chap. 3 of Churchland and Sejnowski [23]), which have evolved into the modern, multi-layer neural network models for deep learning; see, for example, Aggarwal [24] and his interpretation of neural networks as computational graphs.
- Natural and molecular, or DNA, computing; see, for example, Shasha and Lazere [25].
- The Master Algorithm; for a stimulating discussion of "the quest for the ultimate learning machine", see Domingos [26].

When we use the phrase "rubric of algorithm" in subsequent chapters, we mean the broad, overarching umbrella of modern computer science described in this chapter.

References

1. Berlinski, D.: The Advent of the Algorithm: The Idea that Rules the World. Harcourt, New York (2000)
2. Knuth, D.E.: Selected Papers in Computer Science, CSLI Lecture Notes No. 59. Cambridge University Press, Cambridge (1996)
3. Moore, C., Mertens, S.: The Nature of Computation. Oxford University Press, Oxford (2011)
4. Harel, D., Feldman, Y.: Algorithmics: The Spirit of Computing, 3rd edn. Springer, Berlin (2012)
5. Knuth, D.E.: MMIX: A RISC Computer for the New Millennium, vol. 1, Fascicle 1, Addison-Wesley (Pearson Education), Upper Saddle River (2005)
6. Knuth, D.E.: The Art of Computer Programming, Volume 1: Fundamental Algorithms. Addison-Wesley, Reading (1968)
7. Aho, A.V., Hopcroft, J.E., Ullman, J.D.: The Design and Analysis of Computer Algorithms. Addison-Wesley, Reading (1974)
8. Davis, M.D., Weyuker, E.J.: Computability, Complexity, and Languages. Academic Press, New York (1983)
9. Stewart, I.: The Problems of Mathematics. Oxford University Press, Oxford (1987)
10. Garey, M.R., Johnson, D.S.: Computers and Intractability. W.H. Freeman and Company, San Francisco (1979)
11. Nielsen, M.A., Chuang, I.L.: Quantum Computation and Quantum Information. Cambridge University Press, Cambridge (2000)
12. Penrose, R.: The Emperor's New Mind: Concerning Computers, Minds, and the Laws of Physics. Oxford University Press, Oxford (1989)
13. Traub, J.F.: Iterative Methods for the Solution of Equations. Prentice-Hall, Englewood Cliffs (1964)

14. Dasgupta, S., Papadimitriou, C.H., Vazirani, U.: Algorithms. McGraw-Hill, New York (2006)
15. Cormen, T.H., Leiserson, C.E., Rivest, R.L., Stein, C.: Introduction to Algorithms, 4th edn. MIT Press, Cambridge (2022)
16. Gowers, T., et al.: The Princeton Companion to Mathematics. Princeton University Press, Princeton (2008)
17. Wolfram, S.: A New Kind of Science. Wolfram Media Inc., Champaign (2002)
18. Moore, C.: Recursion theory on the reals and continuous-time computation. Theoret. Comput. Sci. **162**, 23–44 (1996)
19. Shannon, C.: Mathematical theory of the differential analyzer. J. Math. Phys. MIT **20**, 337–354 (1941)
20. Nazareth, J.L.: Numerical Algorithmic Science and Engineering. PSIPress, Portland. Freely available at: http://www.math.wsu.edu/faculty/nazareth/NumAlg_19Jul12.pdf (2012)
21. Nazareth, J.L.: Real-number models of computation and HP-memristors: a postscript. http://www.math.wsu.edu/faculty/nazareth/Memristors.pdf (2014)
22. Deutsch, D.: Quantum theory, the Church-Turing principle and the universal quantum computer. Proceedings of the Royal Society of London A **400**, 97–117 (1985)
23. Churchland, P.S., Sejnowski, T.J.: The Computational Brain. The MIT Press, Cambridge, A Bradford Book (1992)
24. Aggarwal, C.C.: Neural Networks and Deep Learning. Springer Nature, Switzerland (2018)
25. Shasha, D., Lazere, C.: Natural Computing. W.W Norton and Company, New York (2010)
26. Domingos, P.: The Master Algorithm: How the Quest for the Ultimate Learning Machine will Remake Our World. Basic Books, New York (2015)

Chapter 4
A Taxonomy of Numerical Problems

4.1 Introduction

In the previous two chapters, we introduced the two thematic pillars, or foundational concepts, of this book: "number" and "algorithm." In combination they provide the means whereby *numerical problems can be solved algorithmically* on an electronic, digital computer, and this *union* can be achieved in two fundamentally different ways.

Speaking metaphorically, one approach brings the foundational concept of a symbol-based algorithm under the "rubric of number." (We use this phrase within quotes in the sense stated at the end of Chap. 2.) This stands in contrast to the other, and indeed complementary, approach of bringing the foundational concept of a symbol-based number under the "rubric of algorithm". (Likewise, we use this phrase in the sense stated at the end of the previous chapter.)

The resulting disciplines, namely, *numerical analysis* within mathematics and *numerical algorithmics* within computer science, will be discussed in the next two chapters. But first we must consider the numerical problems themselves that must be solved by algorithmic means within these two disciplines.

4.2 A "Cubist" Portrait

As in Chap. 1, we shall use an image, or visual icon, to summarize our taxonomy of numerical problems, and once more we shall take our cue from Whitehead [1], *An Introduction to Mathematics*, a masterpiece that we've already encountered in Chap. 2. Let us recall the following from Whitehead [1], which we quoted previously in that chapter (italics mine):

> .... *three notions, of the variable, of form, and of generality, compose a sort of* mathematical trinity, which preside over the whole subject. They all really spring from the same root, namely from the abstract nature of the science.

J. L. Nazareth, *Concise Guide to Numerical Algorithmics*,
SpringerBriefs in Computer Science,
https://doi.org/10.1007/978-3-031-21762-3_4

By way of illustration, consider the linear inequality $ax + by + cz \leq 0$ defined over the reals *R*. Here *x*, *y*, and *z* are the *variables* and a, b, and c are the *parameters*, or *constants*, of the inequality, which has a linear *form* and belongs with greater *generality* to the class of linear inequalities with zero right-hand sides. The parameters in this inequality could be specific real numbers in which case the variables that satisfy it would belong to an identifiable half-space; alternatively, the parameters could be stochastic quantities known only with a given probability distribution, which in turn would induce a probability distribution on the half-spaces to which the variables satisfying the stochastic inequality belong.

Building on Whitehead's "mathematical trinity," let us now characterize numerical problems to be solved algorithmically by using the following partitions of the mathematical entities that serve to define such problems:

- discrete variables vis-à-vis continuous;
- finite-dimensional variables vis-à-vis infinite-dimensional;
- deterministic parameters vis-à-vis stochastic;
- and additionally, problems that are defined by means of a network form, or structure, vis-à-vis problems that are not.

This leads to the "cubist" portrait shown in Fig. 4.1, which is adopted from Nazareth [2, Fig. 10.1], but with labels now added in order to identify particular sub-cubes and slices for use in the discussion below. For example, the label **A** identifies the class of deterministic, continuous and finite-dimensional problems.

4.3 Classes of Numerical Problems

We now give a *few illustrative examples* of numerical problems within each of the "sub-cubes" or "slices" in the figure. These are labeled alphabetically. However, for convenience, the labels **D** and **F** at the back of the cube, which correspond to infinite-dimensional problems, are not shown explicitly, but they are easily deduced: **F** corresponds to problems that are discrete, deterministic and infinite-dimensional; and **D** analogously for problems defined by networks.

4.3.1 A-F: Deterministic Parameters

A. Continuous and Finite-Dimensional: e.g., solving systems of linear equations; the algebraic Eigen-problem; matrix factorizations; optimization problems defined over R^n, for instance, unconstrained nonlinear minimization; linear and non-linear programming; solving systems of nonlinear equations; linear and nonlinear least squares problems.

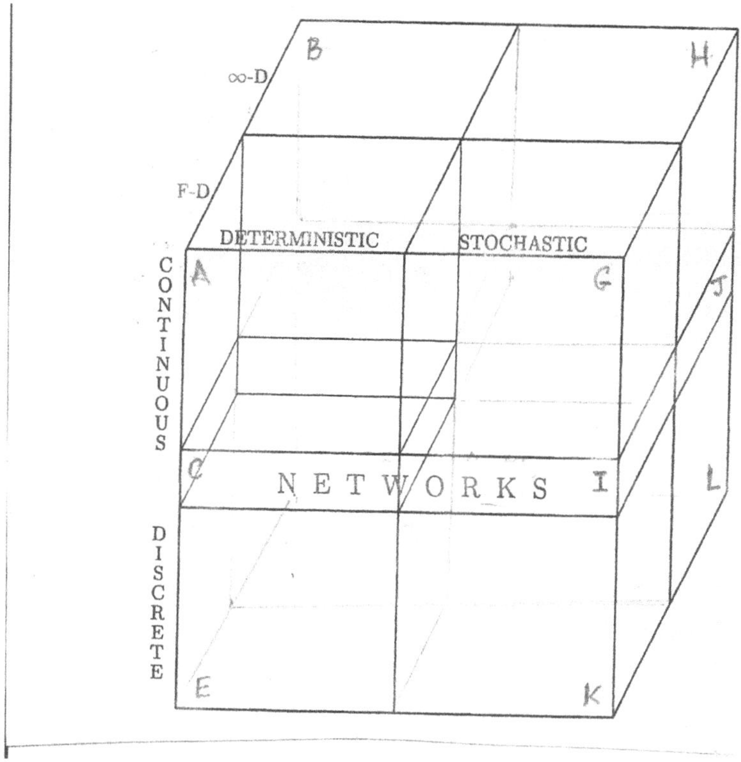

Fig. 4.1 A "Cubist" portrait of numerical problems

B. Continuous and Infinite-Dimensional: e.g., solving ordinary differential equations (ODEs); partial differential equations (PDEs); integral equations; integro-differential equations; variational problems; approximations by splines; quadrature.

C. Finite-Dimensional Networks: e.g., Eulerian and Hamiltonian circuits; shortest path; maximum-flow and minimum-cut; optimal matching and covering; optimal spanning trees; travelling salesman problems; transportation problems; dynamic programming.

D. Infinite-Dimensional Networks: e.g., optimal control problems.

E. Discrete and Finite-Dimensional: e.g., integer programming; 0-1 programming; mixed integer programming.

F. Discrete and Infinite-Dimensional: e.g., numerical problems with denumerably-many unknowns, which are discrete-valued. Such problems may be inequality-constrained and based on infinite matrices or infinite-dimensional discrete operators (viewed as a difference analog of differential equations on the whole axis).

4.3.2 G-L: Stochastic Parameters

G. Continuous and Finite-dimensional: counterparts of problems **A** above, e.g., stochastic programming; recourse problems; problems with chance constraints; Markov decision problems.

H. Continuous and Infinite-Dimensional: counterparts of problems **B** above, e.g., stochastic ODEs; stochastic PDEs.

I. Finite-Dimensional Networks: counterparts of problems **C** above, e.g., stochastic dynamic programming.

J. Infinite-Dimensional Networks: counterparts of problems **D** above, e.g., stochastic optimal control.

K. Discrete and Finite-Dimensional: stochastic counterparts of problems **E** above.

L. Discrete and Infinite-Dimensional: stochastic counterparts of problems **F** above.

4.4 Discussion

With reference to Fig. 4.1, we can now observe the following:

- Problems in category **B** are generally solved via suitable approximations by problems within category **A**. Although the demarcation between these two categories is clear, they nevertheless go hand-in-hand. (The term "discretization" is often used in connection with creating such finite-dimensional approximations, but note that the latter problems remain "continuous," i.e., numerical problems obtained by discretization of an infinite-dimensional counterpart should not be confused with discrete numerical problems, i.e. problems whose variables are discrete-valued.) Furthermore, the deterministic numerical problems in these two categories usually have stochastic counterparts. Thus the "continuous" numerical problems within categories **A**, **B**, **G**, and **H** in the upper half of the figure form a natural grouping.
- Numerical problems in category **E** often occur in combination with numerical problems in category **A**, for example, *mixed integer programming* problems. And problems in category **C** mediate between categories **A** and **E**, because network problems with integer parameters can possess solutions that are integer-valued without that restriction having to be *explicitly imposed* on their variables. Furthermore, and not infrequently, numerical problems can be mixtures of these three categories. And deterministic problems in these categories have stochastic counterparts. Thus numerical problems within categories **A**, **C**, **E**, **G**, **I**, and **K** in the front half of the figure also form a natural grouping.
- In light of the foregoing observations, one can assert that the great "watershed" in numerical computation is more clearly demarcated between *infinite-* and *finite-dimensional* numerical problems than it is between *continuous* and

discrete numerical problems, i.e., between the front and rear halves of Fig. 4.1 than between its upper and lower regions.

- Numerical problems in the remaining categories, namely, **D**, **F**, **J**, and **L** stand apart from the others, but are not uncommon.
- Note that finer distinctions can be made in all the foregoing categories, in particular, between numerical problems that are small, medium or large-scale. This has a marked influence on the design of algorithms and software for solving problems distinguished by their scale.
- It is also worth mentioning explicitly that *algorithms and software for solving numerical linear algebra problems of finite dimension*, ranging from small and dense to very large and sparse, are of central importance to scientific computing, as exemplified by the Turing Award recently given to a distinguished "numerical algorist," Jack Dongarra.
- And finally, we mention two classic references for the categorization of numerical problems, namely, Collatz [3] and Ortega and Rheinboldt [4], both of which contain many sample problems in their introductory chapters.

References

1. Whitehead, A.N.: An Introduction to Mathematics. Henry Holt and Company, New York. Reprinted by Forgotten Books, 2010. www.forgottenbooks.org (1911)
2. Nazareth, J.L.: An Optimization Primer: On Models, Algorithms, and Duality. Springer, New York (2004)
3. Collatz, L.: Functional Analysis and Numerical Mathematics. Academic Press, New York (1966)
4. Ortega, J.M., Rheinboldt, W.C.: Iterative Solution of Nonlinear Equations in Several Variables. Academic Press, New York (1970)

Chapter 5
Numerical Analysis: Algorithm Under the Rubric of Number

5.1 Introduction

In a survey of the discipline of numerical analysis that appeared in the *Princeton Companion to Mathematics* (Gowers et al. [1]), the renowned numerical analyst, Professor Nick Trefethen of Oxford University, makes the following observation:

> Numerical analysis sprang from mathematics; then it spawned the field of computer science. When universities began to found computer science departments in the 1960s, numerical analysts were often in the lead. Now, two generations later, most of them are to be found in mathematics departments. What happened? A part of the answer is that numerical analysts deal with continuous mathematical problems, whereas computer scientists prefer discrete ones, and it is remarkable how wide a gap that can be.

And, in a continuation of these observations, he characterizes modern numerical analysis as follows (italics mine):

> In the 1950s and 1960s, the founding fathers of the field discovered that inexact arithmetic can be a source of danger, causing errors in results that "ought" to be right. The source of such problems is *numerical instability*, that is, the amplification of rounding errors from microscopic to macroscopic scale by certain modes of computation. These men, including Von Neumann, Wilkinson, Forsythe, and Henrici, took pains to publicize the risks of careless reliance on computer arithmetic. These risks are very real, but the message was communicated all too successfully, leading to the widespread impression that the main business of numerical analysis is coping with rounding errors. In fact, *the main business of numerical analysis is designing algorithms that converge quickly;* rounding error analysis, while a part of the discussion, is rarely the central issue. If rounding error vanishes, 90% of numerical analysis would remain.

In light of these observations, one might be tempted to go even so far as to say that, just as Traub [2], Knuth [3], and Harel and Feldman [4] would have preferred that the discipline of computer science be called "algorithmics," so might the name "algorithmic numerics" have been preferable for the discipline of "numerical analysis"; and, correspondingly, "algorithmic numericists" for its practitioners. But, of

J. L. Nazareth, *Concise Guide to Numerical Algorithmics*,
SpringerBriefs in Computer Science,
https://doi.org/10.1007/978-3-031-21762-3_5

course, the traditional designators of "numerical analysis" and "numerical analysts" are now here to stay.

In his 2008 article referenced above, Trefethen further notes that numerical analysis is a discipline that is "built on strong foundations, the mathematical subject of *approximation theory*," and that it has grown into "one of the largest branches of mathematics, the specialty of thousands of researchers who publish in dozens of mathematical journals as well as application journals across the sciences and engineering."

Along similar lines within a classical textbook on numerical analysis whose title, *Analysis of Numerical Methods*, serves to encapsulate the subject, Isaacson and Keller [5] make the following observations (italics mine):

> Our opinion is that the analysis of numerical methods is a broad and challenging mathematical activity whose central theme is the effective constructability of *various kinds of approximations*, ...[and that] deeper studies of numerical methods would *rely heavily on functional analysis*.

Today, the solution of continuous, *infinite-dimensional* numerical problems, i.e., problems defined over *function spaces*, for example, partial-differential equations, systems of ordinary differential equations, integral equations, integrodifferential equations, problems of optimal control, and so on, receives the lion's share of attention from numerical analysts. Such problems are generally solved, in practice, by a reduction to *continuous* problems of *finite* dimension, and thus the latter subject, either self-contained or in the service of solving infinite-dimensional problems, also comprises an important component of numerical analysis. Thus, we observe that numerical analysis deals with numerical problems that occupy the upper half of Fig. 4.1 in Chap. 4 and are identified by the labels **A**, **B**, **G**, and **H** in the figure. Numerical analysts seeks effective algorithms to solve such problems under the "rubric of number," a phrase that is used here in its broadest interpretation, as stated in the conclusion of Chap. 2.

In this brief, ancillary chapter, we outline the theoretical and practical foundations of the discipline of numerical analysis, which today is firmly headquartered within pure and applied mathematics. We do so primarily in order to contrast numerical analysis with the *re*-emergent discipline of numerical algorithmics within computer science, which will be addressed, in detail, in the next chapter.

5.2 Theoretical Foundations of Numerical Analysis

Consider the following, oft-quoted, prescient remarks of John von Neumann made at the dawn of the computer era—see his collected works edited by Taub [6]:

> There exists today a very elaborate system of formal logic, and specifically, of logic applied to mathematics. This is a discipline with many good sides but also serious weaknesses. .... Everybody who has worked in formal logic will confirm that it is one of the most technically refractory parts of mathematics. The reason for this is that it deals with rigid, all-or-none-concepts, and has very little contact with the continuous concept of the real or the complex

> number, that is, with mathematical analysis. Yet analysis is the technically most successful and best-elaborated part of mathematics. Thus formal logic, by the nature of its approach, is cut off from the best cultivated portions of mathematics, and forced into the most difficult terrain into combinatorics.
>
> The theory of automata, of the digital, all-or-none type as discussed up to now, is certainly a chapter in formal logic. It would, therefore, seem that it will have to share this unattractive property of formal logic. It will have to be, from the mathematical point of view, combinatorial rather than analytical.

The repatriation of numerical analysts from computer science to mathematics in the 1990s, as just discussed in the previous section, had an important consequence. The study of fundamental models of computation and complexity developed within theoretical computer science—the so-called "grand unified theory of computation" discussed in Chap. 3—leapfrogged back into mathematics, from whence the subject had originated with mathematical logicians of the 1930s. This development was thanks largely to the work of Fields Medalist Stephen Smale (and his co-workers), who describes his motivation as follows (quoted from the panel discussion in Renegar et al. [7], italics mine):

> A lot of my motivation in spending so much time trying to understand numerical analysis is to help my own ideas about how to define an algorithm. It seems to me that it is important [if one is] to understand the subject of numerical analysis to make a definition of algorithm .... *It is the main object of study of numerical analysis* and to have a definition of it so someone can look at all algorithms or a class of algorithms is an important line of understanding.

5.2.1 The BCSS Model of Computation

In an ensuing, landmark monograph, Blum et al. [8] presented a computational model (BCSS) of *great generality*—abstract machines defined over mathematical rings and fields—and used it to develop a theory of *computational complexity*, in particular, over the real and complex numbers. (Furthermore, when Z_2, i.e., the integers modulus 2, are used for the underlying structure, then the model is capable of capturing the classical theory of computation considered in Chap. 3.) The foregoing developments led also to the establishment of the Foundations of Computational Mathematics (FoCM) Society to foster such activities.

The main features of a BCSS machine are as follows:

- A *state space* S_M;
- an *input space* I_M;
- an *output space* O_M;
- *a finite, connected graph defined by a set of labeled nodes and directed edges between nodes.*

In a *finite-dimensional* machine (FD-BCSS), the state space S_M, the input space I_M, and the output space O_M, are identified with the Euclidean spaces R^m, R^n and R^l, respectively, where *m, n,* and *l* are positive integers. The nodes of the finite, connected, and directed graph have unique labels, denoted *generically* by β. And the execution sequence of the machine is defined by this directed graph, starting at the *INPUT NODE* (see below), and following a path within the directed graph, which terminates at an *OUTPUT NODE* (again see below).

The machine has four basic types of nodes as follows:

1. *COMPUTATION NODE:* A BCSS machine has a single, generic node for performing arithmetic operations that is defined by associating a rational map with the node. (This rational map, say g: $R^m \rightarrow R^m$, has m components, $g_j(x) = p_j(x)/q_j(x)$, $j = 1, \ldots, m$, and p_j and q_j are polynomials. Each such polynomial has m variables and is of finite degree $\leq d$. The polynomials, in turn, can be defined as the sum of monomials.) After completion of the operation, proceed to the node's successor β in the directed graph.
2. *BRANCH NODE:* Compute the result, say r, of an associated rational functional that maps the state space to the reals, i.e., $S_M \rightarrow R$. If $r \geq 0$ then go to a different node identified by a label, say β', which is specified with this node. Otherwise, the execution sequence is defined by the successor β.
3. *INPUT NODE:* A *linear*, or matrix, map from $I_M \rightarrow S_M$ is used to initialize the state space. An input node can only occur once at the start of the execution sequence, i.e., at any other node, its successor node β cannot be set to the unique label associated with the input node.
4. *OUTPUT NODE:* A *linear*, or matrix, map from $S_M \rightarrow O_M$ serves to generate the output. Then the BCSS machine halts, i.e., β is null for each output node.

The finite-dimensional BCSS model is further refined into the so-called *normal form* by using the integers 1, 2, ..., N for the labels associated with the nodes of the directed graph and with the input node given the label β = 1. There is also only one output node and it is given the unique label N. (Some additional simplifications of the *BRANCH NODE* are made that need not concern us here.)

As an aside, one can view an FD-BCSS machine through the lens of the random-access (RAM) and Turing machine (TM) models of computation described in Chap. 3 by making the following identifications: the state space $S_M = R^m$ is viewed as a "read–write memory" that consists of a finite number of registers, numbered 1, 2, 3, …,m, which define their "addresses." Each register can store an arbitrary real number (including zero). Similarly, the input space $I_M = R^n$ and output space $O_M = R^l$ are viewed as input and output "tapes," which, respectively, consist of n and l contiguous cells, each of which can store a real number. And each uniquely labeled node of the directed graph can be converted into "primitive program lines" defined by TM-like tuples as follows:

(Label, Operation-Code, Address Field, Successor Label(s))

where 'Label' is defined by the unique label given to the corresponding node, the 'Operation-Code' is defined by one of the four types of nodes described above, 'Address-Field' is defined by the rational map or functional associated with the node, and the 'Successor Label(s)' correspond to a BRANCH node's two possible successors or the unique successor for the COMPUTATION and INPUT nodes, and null for the OUTPUT node. An FD-BCSS 'program' would then consist of an ordered sequence of such primitive program lines, akin to a RAM program, and is executed analogously.

Returning now to the FD-BCSS model, Blum et al. [8] note the following:

> A pillar of the classical theory of computation is the existence of a *universal* Turing machine, a machine that can compute any computable function. This theoretical construct foretold and provides a foundation for the modern general-purpose computer. .... If we wish to construct universal machines over the reals, and to develop a general theory of computation, we are led naturally to consider machines that can handle finite but *unbounded* sequences [as contrasted with the finite-dimensional restrictions of the state and other spaces of the FD-BCSS machine]. This in fact is closer to Turing's original approach.

In their *general*, or uniform, version of the BCSS machine, the input, output, and state spaces correspond to the aforementioned "finite but unbounded sequences" of real numbers, i.e., R^{∞} defined as the disjoint union of R^n, $n \geq 0$ and R_{∞} defined as an associated bi-infinite direct sum space. For further detail on this extension and the resulting universal machine, see Blum et al. [8]. And an interpretation of the general BCSS machine that seeks to place it within the Turing-RAM tradition can be found in Nazareth [9].

The BCSS model provided the basis for a deep study of the foundations of computing over the reals and of the computational complexity of real-number algorithms. But Stephen Smale has also expressed the following reservations about the BCSS model as it applies to the day-to-day work of numerical analysts (quoted again from the panel discussion in Renegar et al. [7]):

> .....numerical analysis does not need these things. It doesn't need a model of computation. But on the other hand, I think that [it] will develop. It's going to develop anyway, and it is going to develop probably more in parallel with existing analysis numerical. Numerical analysis will do very fine without it. But in the long run, these ideas from geometry and foundations will give a lot of insights and understanding of numerical analysis.

5.3 Practical Foundations of Numerical Analysis

5.3.1 *The IEEE 754 Floating-Point Standard*

A practical model of computation based on axiomatized, finite-precision, floating-point arithmetic was described in Chap. 3. Recall its key feature upon which the error analysis of numerical algorithms depends, namely, that

$$\mathrm{fl}(x \,\#\, y) = (x \,\#\, y)(1 + \mu),$$

where x and y are any two *representable* floating-point numbers, '#' denotes any one of the four basic arithmetic operations, 'fl' denotes the result of that floating-point arithmetic operation, and $|\mu| \leq 2^{-t}$, where the latter quantity is often called a unit in the last place (ulp). Note that μ will vary depending upon the operation # and the operands x and y, but the *bound* on $|\mu|$ is, in each case, the same number (ulp).

The foregoing is an important foundation for modern numerical analysis in practice. It is the basis of the fundamental works of Wilkinson [10, 11], who developed a number of subtle and beautiful concepts, including backward error analysis (coupled with perturbation theory), the stability of algorithms, and the ill-conditioning of problems.

The Turing-award winner, William Kahan, spearheaded the creation of the IEEE 754 standardization for implementing the foregoing axiomatic floating-point model in the arithmetic units of today's computers. A conventional floating-point number is represented by a word length of, say, n bits. This consists of a single sign bit b; a set of es bits containing an unsigned binary integer, which represents a shifted or biased exponent e', where $0 \leq e' \leq (2^{es} - 1)$, and from which the bias can be removed to obtain the exponent e (a negative, zero, or positive integer); and the remaining $t = (n\text{-}es\text{-}1)$ bits, which represent a normalized mantissa (significand, fraction) f, and where normalized means the leading binary digit of f is 1. Thus a number x is given by $x = (-1)^b f\ 2^e$. The number of bits within each of the various components that define the finite-precision floating-point number x is fixed. For instance, a 64-bit number has a single sign bit, $es = 11$ bits for the exponent, and $t = 52$ bits for the mantissa. The arithmetic operations are implemented to obey the axiomatized model described in Chap. 3.

This IEEE standard has been such a success that it has in a sense closed the book on the subject of floating-point arithmetic and enabled, for example, the following remarks of the eminent numerical analyst, Gene Golub, as reported in a panel discussion in Renegar et al. [7].

> I'd like to say something about floating-point arithmetic .....It is important to know, a few people should know it perhaps. But I don't consider it a part of the mainstream of numerical analysis any longer. Perhaps one needs to know the model. But along with Wilkinson error analysis it isn't the mainstream of what we call scientific computing today.

They echo the observations of Nick Trefethen which we have quoted above.

5.3.2 *The Chebfun Model*

In a development that is as significant for numerical analysis as was the earlier BCSS theoretical model and the IEEE 754 standard, Trefethen [12] and his co-workers have proposed a practical model for numerical computation on *functions* instead of numbers. He describes it as follows (italics his):

> Chebfun is built on an analogy. To work with real numbers on a computer, we typically approximate them to 16 digits by finite bit strings: *floating-point numbers*, with an associated concept of *rounding* at each step of a calculation. To work with functions, Chebfun approximates them to 16 digits by polynomials (or piecewise polynomials) of finite degree: Chebyshev expansions, with an associated concept of rounding. Thus the key to numerical

> computation with functions is the generalization of the ideas of floating-point approximation and rounding from numbers to functions.

Recall our result or axiomatic floating-point arithmetic on numbers in the previous subsection:

$$\mathrm{fl}(x \# y) = (x \# y)(1 + \mu), \quad \text{where } |\mu| \leq \text{ulp}$$

where x and y are representable, floating-point numbers.

This can be re-expressed as

$$\begin{aligned} \mathrm{fl}(x \# y) = x^* \# y^* \quad &\text{where } \left|x - x^*\right|/|x| \leq \text{ ulp} \\ &\text{and } \left|y - y^*\right|/|y| \leq \text{ ulp}, \end{aligned}$$

and we thus observe that the arithmetic operations are *backward stable.*

In the Chebfun model, *functions have an analogous representation* called chebfuns as described in the quotation above. If f and g are chebfuns, then the Chebfun model permits operations on them such as $+$, $-$, $\times$, and /, which we collectively represented above by #, as well as other operations, e.g., exp. The intention is not that such computations are exact. Instead the aim of the model is to achieve an analogue of the foregoing floating-point operations, but now for *functions*, namely,

$$\begin{aligned} \mathrm{fl}(f \# g) = f^* \# g^* \quad &\text{with } \left|\left|f - f^*\right|\right|/||f|| \leq \text{C ulp}, \\ &\left|\left|g - g^*\right|\right|/||g|| \leq C \text{ ulp}, \end{aligned}$$

where C is a small constant and ||.|| is a suitable norm. Thus, as Trefethen [12] explains, the aim of the Chebfun model is *normwise backward stable computation of functions.*

For further detail on the Chebfun model, see Trefethen [12], who concludes his overview article as follows:

> ….the deeper point of this article has been to put forward a vision that is not tied specifically to Chebyshev expansions or to other details of Chebfun. The vision is that by the use of adaptive high-accuracy numerical approximations of functions, computational systems can be built that "feel symbolic but run at the speed of numerics".

Once could say that this captures the very spirit of the discipline of numerical analysis!

References

1. Gowers, T., et al.: The Princeton Companion to Mathematics. Princeton University Press, Princeton, New Jersey (2008)
2. Traub, J.F.: Iterative Methods for the Solution of Equations. Prentice-Hall, Englewood Cliffs (1964)

3. Knuth, D.E.: Selected Papers in Computer Science, CSLI Lecture Notes No. 59. Cambridge University Press, Cambridge (1996)
4. Harel, D., Feldman, Y.: Algorithmics: The Spirit of Computing, 3rd edn. Springer, Berlin (2012)
5. Isaacson, E., Keller, H.B.: Analysis of Numerical Methods. Wiley, New York (1966)
6. Taub, A.H. (ed.): Collected Works, vol. V, pp. 288–328. Macmillan, London (von Neumann, J., The general and logical theory of automata) (1961)
7. Renegar, J., Shub, M., Smale, S. (eds.): Mathematics of Numerical Analysis. American Mathematical Society, Providence, Rhode Island (1996)
8. Blum, L. Cucker, F., Shub, M., Smale, S.: Complexity and Real Computation. Springer, New York (with a foreword by R.M. Karp) (1998)
9. Nazareth, J.L.: Numerical Algorithmic Science and Engineering. PSIPress, Portland. Freely available at: http://www.math.wsu.edu/faculty/nazareth/NumAlg_19Jul12.pdf (2012)
10. Wilkinson, J.H.: Rounding Errors in Algebraic Processes. Prentice-Hall, New Jersey (1963)
11. Wilkinson, J.H.: The Algebraic Eigenvalue Problem. Clarendon Press, Oxford (1965)
12. Trefethen, L.N.: Computing numerically with functions instead of numbers. Comm. ACM **58**(10), 91–97 (2015)

Chapter 6
Numerical Algorithmics: Number Under the Rubric of Algorithm

6.1 Introduction

Let us recall some observations from previous chapters, namely, the "grand unified theory of computation," which provided the theoretical foundations for computer science and was developed by mathematical logicians during the 1930s; the computer revolution, which began during the 1940s with the invention of the electronic, digital computer; and the creation of academic departments of computer science within universities worldwide during the late 1950s and the 1960s.

When the discipline of computer science thereby came into existence, a foundational pillar was knowledge of an array of algorithms, mostly of a numeric nature and associated with the names of famous mathematicians of the past, for example, Euclid, Newton, Euler, Fourier, Gauss, and Cauchy. These classical numerical algorithms were natural candidates for problem-solving on a electronic, digital computer. Another noteworthy application was George Dantzig's linear programming (LP) model—nowadays also called linear optimization—and his simplex algorithm for efficiently solving such LPs, which were invented during the mid-1940s and evolved in tandem with advances in electronic computing. In consequence, mathematicians identified with the fields of numerical analysis and optimization played a central role in the creation of the computer science discipline. Departments of mathematics continued to field strong groups in numerical analysis, but many numerical analysts, especially those concerned with solving problems defined over real numerical spaces of *finite* dimension, transitioned to newly-created academic departments of computer science during the 1960s.

A central concern of such numerical analysts in the early days was how to cope with the limitations of floating-point arithmetic. Here the fundamental works of Wilkinson [1, 2], who earlier was a close collaborator of Alan Turing, provided basic guidelines and a number of subtle and beautiful concepts: backward-error analysis in conjunction with perturbation theory; the stability of algorithms; and the ill-conditioning of numerical problems. But these developments simultaneously

J. L. Nazareth, *Concise Guide to Numerical Algorithmics*,
SpringerBriefs in Computer Science,
https://doi.org/10.1007/978-3-031-21762-3_6

served to fix an image of numerical analysis in the eyes of other computer scientists, who sometimes tended to look down on work of the error-analysis variety (see, in particular, the essay of Kahan [3]). Computer science had begun rapidly to move away from computations involving numbers—so-called "number crunching"—and toward the manipulation of discrete bits and bytes of digital information. The discipline centered on the "care and feeding of computers," namely, subjects like data structures, programming languages, operating systems, machine organization, theory of computation, artificial intelligence, and so on.

Numerical computation within computer science began increasingly to focus on solving problems of a *discrete or combinatorial* nature. But it is important to note that continuous problems, and *especially problems defined over a real-number space of finite dimension,* also fall centrally within the province of computer science. They arise frequently in conjunction with discrete numerical problems, good examples being provided by mixed integer programming (linear, nonlinear, and stochastic), network-flow programming, and dynamic programming.

The downgrading of numerical analysis as a subfield of computer science (CS) and its repatriation to mathematics, as noted in Chap. 5, had a deleterious consequence for CS. It left largely unfinished the task of building a solid theoretical and practicable foundation for numerical computation *within CS as it relates to real numbers,* one that is well integrated with the classical models of computer science described in Chap. 3. During the earlier period when numerical analysts had a closer affiliation with computer science, this objective was achieved, but only in a very limited way, albeit practically important, through the development and study of the finite-precision, floating-point model of computation and its associated round-off error analysis, as we have described in Chaps. 3 and 5.

The present chapter discusses the means whereby this downgrading of numeric, and in particular real-number, computation within CS can be remedied. We first define and present the rationale for explicitly identifying a discipline within computer science, which we term *numerical algorithmic science and engineering (NAS&E),* or more compactly, *numerical algorithmics.* It is the counterpart within computer science of the discipline of numerical analysis within mathematics described in Chap. 5. We then briefly survey some recently proposed models of real-number computation that can contribute to the task of building a solid theoretical and practical foundation for NAS&E. Finally, the context and organization of NAS&E from the standpoints of education and research within the CS curriculum are considered in detail. It is our hope that this re-emerging discipline within CS will reoccupy the region within academic departments of computer science that was left vacant following the repatriation of numerical analysts to mathematics described in Chap. 5. The complementary disciplines of numerical analysis, now headquartered within pure and applied mathematics, and numerical algorithmics (NAS&E), potentially headquartered within computer science, would provide an effective platform for the investigation of the problems and models of science and engineering by means of the modern computer, a modus operandi that is known today as scientific computing, or computational science and engineering.

6.2 Definition and Rationale for Numerical Algorithmics

Let us begin by explicitly identifying the discipline within computer science that is the desired counterpart of numerical analysis within mathematics:

> Numerical Algorithmic Science and Engineering (NAS&E), or more compactly Numerical Algorithmics, is the theoretical and empirical study and the practical implementation and application of algorithms for solving **finite-dimensional problems of a numeric nature** that may or may not be defined by an underlying network/graph structure and whose variables are either discrete-valued, or continuous over the reals, or, and as is often the case, a combination of the two. This discipline lies within computer science, and it supports the modern modus operandi of computational science and engineering, or scientific computing.

With reference to Fig. 4.1 and the discussion in Chap. 4, we see that NAS&E addresses numerical problems in the front half of that figure, namely, the problem categories identified by the labels **A**, **C**, **E**, **G**, **I**, and **K**. Earlier we noted that the discipline of numerical analysis within mathematics addresses "continuous" problem categories in the upper half of the figure, corresponding to the label **A**, **B**, **G**, and **H**. Thus numerical algorithmics (NAS&E) within computer science, as defined above, and numerical analysis within mathematics overlap with one another in the domain of continuous, finite-dimensional numerical problem-solving, namely, the regions labeled **A** and **G**, but often with significant differences in emphasis and the types of algorithmic issues that are addressed, e.g., large-scale, sparse, highly-structured, and so on.

As we have stated previously in Chap. 4, NAS&E seeks to bring the concept of symbol-based number, as presented in Chap. 2, under the "rubric of algorithm," where the latter phrase is used in the sense stated at the end of Chap. 3, namely, the full umbrella of the computer science discipline. We suggest that specialists in NAS&E be called *numerical algorists*, the counterpart within computer science of numerical analysts within mathematics (see also Nazareth [4]). The word "algorist" has a proud tradition, stretching back to the great Persian mathematician Al-Khowarizm (9th Century, A.D.) from whose name and works both "algorithm" and "algebra" are derived. It is often said that the words "algorithmic thinking" characterize the field of computer science—see, in particular, the 1985 essay "Algorithmic thinking and mathematical thinking" of Donald Knuth that can be found, in expanded form, in Knuth [5]—and, likewise, one could characterize numerical algorithmics (NAS&E) within computer science as "algorithmic thinking applied to finite-dimensional, discrete and/or continuous numerical problems."

Let us now very briefly survey the theoretical and practical foundations of NAS&E, before turning to a detailed discussion of the content and organization of this discipline.

6.3 Theoretical Foundations

6.3.1 Real-Number Models in the Turing Tradition

The famed computer scientist Stephen Cook and his student Mark Braverman have promulgated the "bit-model" for scientific computing, which seeks to incorporate real-numbers into the model while remaining, as closely as possible, within the Turing tradition. In essence, a real-number function $f(x)$ is computable in their approach if there exists an algorithm which, given a good *rational* approximation to x, finds a good *rational* approximation to $f(x)$. And Braverman and Cook [6] contrast their "bit-model" with the "algebraic" approach, which the late Traub [7], another eminent computer scientist, has characterized as follows (italics mine):

> A central dogma of computer science is that the Turing machine is the appropriate abstraction of the digital computer. .... I argue here that physicists [and indeed all scientists and engineers] should consider the real-number model of computation as more appropriate and useful for scientific computation. .... The crux of this model is that one can *store and perform arithmetic operations and comparisons on real numbers* exactly and at unit cost.

A "magnitude-based" formalization of Traub's approach, but with *logarithmic costs* for its basic arithmetic operations, is presented in Nazareth [8]. It *reconceptualizes the floating-point number system* so as to permit computation with real numbers within the standard and well-known RAM/RASP model of theoretical computer science. In the resulting, so-called CD-RAM/RASP model of computation, a real number is defined by a mantissa and an exponent, the former being represented by an *analog* "magnitude," or A-bit, and the latter by a finite, digital sequence of unary (or binary) bits. Arithmetic operations between A-bits are defined *abstractly* by means of geometric-based operations on magnitudes, which are now potentially implementable, in practice, through the use of HP-memristors—for details, see Nazareth [9].

6.4 Practical Foundations

6.4.1 Floats

The well-known finite-precision floating-point model and associated analysis based on the classic work of Wilkinson [1] and the IEEE 754 standard have been discussed in previous chapters. Here we simply note that the model can be fully embraced by the foregoing abstract, real-number models in the Turing tradition and viewed very simply as their *coarsening for practical purposes.* In other words, the floating-point model can be *subsumed* within the "grand unified theory of computer science," once this theory has been suitably broadened to incorporate real-number models of computation.

6.4.2 Unums and Posits

An alternative universal number (unum) arithmetic framework was developed recently in Gustafson [10, 11] and Gustafson and Yonemoto [12], and is summarized in this last reference as follows:

> The **unum** (universal **num**ber) arithmetic framework has several forms. The original "Type I" unum is a superset of IEEE 754 Standard floating-point format...; it uses a "ubit" at the end of the fraction to indicate whether a real number is an exact float or lies in the open interval between floats. While the sign, exponent, and fraction bit fields *take their definition from IEEE 754, the exponent and fraction field lengths vary* automatically, from a single bit up to some maximum set by the user. Type-I unums provide a compact way to express *interval arithmetic*, but their variable length demands extra management. They can duplicate IEEE float behavior, via an explicit rounding function.
>
> The "Type II" unum abandons compatibility with IEEE floats, permitting a clean mathematical design based on the projective reals.

Finally, "Type III" unums, also called *posits,* were proposed by Gustafson and Yonemoto [12] in a radical departure from the floating-point system and its associated IEEE 754 standard. Within a posit representation of n bits, the leading sign bit b is defined as in a floating-point number. A posit has exponent e and fraction f akin to a floating-point number described above, but unlike the IEEE 754 standard, the exponent and fraction parts of a posit do *not* have fixed length. And a posit has an additional category of bits, known as the *regime,* which is also of variable length.

An excellent mathematical account can be found in "*Anatomy of a posit number*" by Cook [13], which is derived, in turn, from Gustafson and Yonemoto [12]. Following the sign bit, the regime has first priority and is defined by a *unary* sequence of length say m, comprising either all zeros or all ones, where m can range from a single bit to as many as $n - 1$. If the regime is defined by a sequence of 0's then set $k = -m$, otherwise, if defined by 1's, set $k = m - 1$. The remaining bits, if any, up to a maximum allowable number specified by an exogenous parameter es, define the exponent, a non-negative integer e, s.t. $0 \leq e \leq (2^{es} - 1)$. If there are still bits left after the exponent bits, the rest go into the normalized fraction f defined as 1+ the fraction bits interpreted as following a binary point. (e.g., if the fraction bits are 10011, then $f = 1.10011$ in binary.) The posit x is then defined as follows: $x = (-1)^b f\ 2^{(e+kw)}$ where $w = 2^{es}$. More explanatory detail can be found in Cook [13] who observes that "the primary advantage of posits is the ability to get more precision or dynamic range out of a given number of bits," i.e., posits have "tapered precision [in the sense that] numbers near 1 have more precision, while extremely big numbers and extremely small numbers have less." He notes also that "there's only one zero for posit numbers, unlike IEEE floats that have two kinds of zero, one positive and one negative," and that "there's also only one infinite posit number. For that reason you could say that posits represent projective real numbers rather than extended real numbers. IEEE floats have two kinds of infinities, positive and negative, as well as several kinds of non-numbers."

However, in order to recover some of the beautiful, Wilkinson-type error analysis associated with the finite-precision, floating-point model, in particular, backward error analysis vis-à-vis perturbation theory when seeking to establish the numerical stability of an algorithm vis-à-vis the numerical stability of the problem that it is solving—for example, an arbitrary triangular system of linear equations with non-zero diagonal elements by forward- or back-substitution (see Nazareth [14], Sect. 4.4)—it may be necessary to have a pre-specified, *lower bound* on the number of bits, say t, assigned to the normalized mantissa (fraction), thus leaving the remaining $(n - t)$ bits for the sign, regime, exponent, and possibly additional higher-order bits for the mantissa, as described above. But this negates some of the characteristics of posits mentioned in the previous paragraph and is a subject that requires further exploration. For further discussion of floating-point vis-à-vis posits, see Greenbaum [15]. More recently, an insightful, in-depth study of posits is given by De Dinechin et al. [16]. They emphasize the serious drawback of posits mentioned above as follows:

> A very useful feature of standard floating-point arithmetic is that, barring underflow/overflow, the relative error due to rounding (and therefore the relative error of all correctly-rounded functions, including the arithmetic operations and the square root) is bounded by a small value 2^{-t} where t is the precision of the format. Almost all numerical analysis ... is based on this very useful property. [For consistency with the earlier discussion in Chap. 3, the quantity 'p' in this quotation has been replaced by 't'.]

De Dinechin et al. [16] note that "this is no longer true with posits" and, in consequence, "numerical analysis has to be rebuilt from scratch." A remedy might be the option of imposing a pre-specified, lower-bound on the number of mantissa (fraction) bits of posits as mentioned above.

For the reasons stated above, it seems very unlikely that posits and unums will replace the IEEE 754 standard created by the Turing-award winner, William Kahan, but they will have appeal for specialty computer applications, for example, within machine and deep learning.

6.5 NAS&E: Content and Organization

The foregoing developments begin to lay a foundation for NAS&E within computer science that conforms to its traditional roots. While such theoretical and practicable foundational models are consequential, the primary focus of NAS&E must always remain on the *scientific study* of the finite-dimensional, discrete and/or continuous, algorithms themselves and their *engineered implementation* at all levels. (For a detailed discussion of hierarchical levels of implementation of numerical algorithms, see Nazareth [17].)

Early and classic works along these lines are Wilkinson [1, 2] and Dantzig [18]. The former is the definitive, path-breaking work on solving systems of linear equations and the algebraic Eigenproblem over real (and complex) finite-dimensional spaces. In reference to this work and quoting again from the aforementioned panel discussion in Renegar et al. [19], Beresford Parlett, one of the world's leading experts in matrix computations and numerical analysis, notes the following:

> Even advancing more in time in the field of matrix computations to the sort of bible written by Wilkinson in the 1950s and 60s, he hardly proves a theorem in the book. I've heard people in the audience criticizing the book, because they say it is very inconvenient to use as a reference. The subject really isn't organized very neatly. I think that is actually a true criticism. You sort of have to swallow it whole.

But this gets to the heart of the matter. Wilkinson [2], the book mentioned in the above quotation, is an inspired work that follows a very different paradigm for presenting its algorithmic material, one that has much more in common with the sciences and engineering than it does with mathematics. It represents quintessential NAS&E. And the same can be said of the 1963 classic of Dantzig [18], *Linear Programming and Extensions*, which was published in the same early period and is another of the crown jewels of NAS&E.

A wide variety of beautiful and powerful algorithms and algorithmic principles for finite-dimensional equation-solving (linear and nonlinear and often of very large scale) and for finite-dimensional, discrete and/or continuous optimization (linear, non-linear, integer, network, dynamic, stochastic, etc.) have since been discovered and studied in a similar vein; for example, max-flow/min-cut, central path-following, matrix factorization (LU, QR, SVD, etc.) and updating, conjugate gradients, quasi-Newton, the duality principle, Nelder-Mead simplex, branch-and-bound, genetic algorithms, bipartite matching/covering, algorithms based on homotopies, Newton-Cauchy framework, Dantzig-Wolfe decomposition of linear programs, and so on, to randomly name but a few. For further detail, see, for example, Moore and Mertens [20] or Nazareth [21, 22].

Turning to the engineering aspect of NAS&E, an outstanding illustration is given by the relevant "recipes" of Press et al. [23]. The engineering of (often highly-complex) implementations of numerical algorithms in a particular computer language and computing environment and the development of appropriate tools that undergird such implementations are an integral part of the NAS&E discipline. For example, Matlab, Python, dialects of C and Fortran, MPI, and so on, are a vital part of the toolkit for implementing algorithms and a numerical algorist should not be merely a competent user of such tools, but should also have some knowledge of what lies "under the hood." Thus, in addition to the mathematical training needed to study finite-dimensional, discrete and/or continuous numerical algorithms, a trained numerical algorist must be cognizant of the techniques that go into the creation of complex data structures, programming languages, compilers and interpreters, operating systems, basic machine design, and so on, subjects at the heart of an education in computer science. The development of implementations and high-quality mathematical software would be a highly respectable activity within NAS&E and academically recognized and rewarded, just as is the case with the creation of non-numeric software within present-day computer science. It is worth noting that the writing of a large piece of mathematical software is as challenging a task as proving a mathematical convergence or rate-of-convergence theorem—harder, perhaps, because the computer is an unrelenting taskmaster.

Why change horses in midstream by introducing new nomenclature rather than simply retaining the previous term "numerical analysis"? The answer is that an educational and research curriculum for numerical algorithmics (NAS&E) within computer science differs significantly in character from its numerical analysis counterpart within mathematics. Let us illustrate this point by outlining an introductory course in NAS&E, which could be structured along the following lines:

1. *Algorithmic Foundations*: 1a: Introduction to the formal notion of algorithm and universal machine and the "grand unified theory of computation" (cf. Chap. 3). 1b: Introduction to the fundamental notion of number (cf. Chap. 2). 1c: Bringing "number" under the rubric of "algorithm" via an introduction to "real-number," abstract models of computation and their practical versions, in particular, the standard finite-precision, floating-point and recently-proposed posit-unum arithmetic systems (cf. Chaps. 3 and 5 and the earlier discussion in this chapter).
2. *Numerical Algorithmic Science:* 2a: A selection of some of the beautiful algorithms and algorithmic principles of finite-dimensional, discrete and continuous numerical computing—see, for example, the ones that were listed earlier in this section. 2b: Applications to realistic numerical problems—an excellent source of applications are now available within computer science, for example, Google's page-ranking algorithm, which is related to the algebraic Eigenproblem, and the use of various optimization algorithms and matrix factorizations within machine and deep learning; see also Solomon [24]. 2c: Some exposure to theoretical convergence and rate-of-convergence analysis, but with much greater emphasis being placed on numerical experimentation with algorithms taught in the foregoing item 2a, using, for example, Matlab or some other convenient computer language; see Nazareth [25] for an illustration. And for a *quintessential case study* in numerical algorithmic science, see Nazareth [26], *The Newton-Cauchy Framework: A Unified Approach to Unconstrained Nonlinear Minimization.*
3. *Numerical Algorithmic Engineering:* 3a: A discussion of practical aspects of implementation, for example, data structures, choice of programming language, and so on—see, for example, Nazareth [14]. 3b: The CS techniques and "under the hood" design of systems like Matlab or Mathematica used for numerical experimentation in item 2c above. And for a *quintessential case study* in numerical algorithmic engineering, see Nazareth [27], *DLP and Extensions: An Optimization Model and Decision Support System* (and its appendices, Nazareth [28, 29]).

This is quite different in content from a standard introductory course on numerical analysis within a mathematics or applied mathematics department—see any of the numerous textbooks available, e.g., Kahaner et al. [30] or Greenbaum and Chartier [31]—which generally begins with an introduction to floating-point computer arithmetic, basic roundoff error-analysis and the numerical solution of systems of linear equations via stabilized Gaussian elimination, and then rapidly moves on to other topics such as polynomial interpolation, quadrature, divided-differences, ordinary and partial differential equation-solving, Monte Carlo methods, Fourier transforms, and so on, and interleaved with optimization-oriented topics like finding the roots of nonlinear equations and the minima of nonlinear functions, in one and several dimensions.

An introductory course in NAS&E within computer science at the graduate or advanced undergraduate level, such as the one outlined above, would typically be followed by a sequence of other courses providing more in-depth coverage. This sequence would take its place alongside course sequences in the standard areas of computer science, for example, data structures, automata theory and formal languages, compiler and interpreter design, operating systems, basic machine design, artificial intelligence, and so on. The NAS&E course sequence would simply be another available arrow in the computer science quiver!

The mathematical background required for NAS&E within CS would be knowledge of linear algebra and calculus, or basic analysis. One cannot expect a computer science student at the undergraduate or graduate level to be conversant with functional analysis, which is an essential prerequisite for any in-depth study of numerical analysis. However, nothing would prevent a student of NAS&E within computer science from broadening his/her training through course offerings in numerical analysis (as well as functional analysis and complex analysis, if needed) from a mathematics or an applied mathematics department. This is analogous to a student of basic machine design within computer science looking to course offerings of an electrical engineering department in seeking to obtain more in-depth instruction in machine hardware.

The creation of small-scale, informally-structured NAS&E research centers within academic departments of computer science can further facilitate the above educational and research objectives. This is discussed in more detail in Nazareth [8].

6.6 Conclusion

Looking now to a more distant horizon, it is appropriate to close this chapter and our book with a second observation, which is taken again from Trefethen's survey of numerical analysis in Gowers et al. [32]. He has anticipated the emergence of NAS&E as a sub-discipline within the field of computer science as follows (italics mine):

> ....the *computer science of numerical analysis is of crucial importance,* and I would like to end with a prediction that emphasizes this side of the subject... . In a world where several algorithms are known for solving every problem, we increasingly find that the most robust computer program will be one that has diverse capabilities at its disposal and deploys them adaptively on the fly. In other words, numerical computation is increasingly deployed in intelligent control loops. I believe this process will continue, just as has happened in many other areas of technology, removing scientists from further details of their computations but offering steadily growing power in exchange. I expect that most of the numerical computer programs of 2050 will be 99% intelligent "wrapper" and just 1% actual "algorithm," if such a distinction makes sense. Hardly anyone will know how they work, and they will be extraordinarily powerful and reliable, and will often deliver results of guaranteed accuracy.

Numerical algorithmics (NAS&E) as delineated in the previous sections of this chapter can be viewed as the aforementioned "computer science of numerical analysis." Our hope is that it will begin to reoccupy the region within academic departments of computer science that was left vacant following the repatriation of numerical analysts to mathematics (as described within Trefethen's observations within his article in Gowers et al. [32], which were quoted previously at the beginning of Chap. 5).

NAS&E is the conduit into computer science of the fundamental concept of "number" drawn from mathematics; see also Chaitin [33] and other references given there for an extensive treatment of *computable numbers* from both a philosophical and a mathematical perspective.

And NAS&E would serve as a bridge between computer science and the natural sciences and engineering, because new and effective algorithms are often first invented by engineers and scientists to solve particular problems, and only later subjected to a more rigorous mathematical and computational analysis.

In conclusion, NAS&E within computer science and numerical analysis within mathematics would *complement* one another and provide *an improved environment for cooperation* in the service of numerical computation. The two disciplines, in conjunction, would provide an effective platform to support the modern modus operandi known as scientific computing, or computational science and engineering, as it seeks to address the "grand challenge" problems of our modern era, for example, the mystery of protein-folding (recently beginning to be unraveled via AI/deep-learning), the intriguing near optimality of the genetic code, and the nature of the relationships between algorithmic computation, human consciousness, and the operations of the brain.

References

1. Wilkinson, J.H.: Rounding Errors in Algebraic Processes. Prentice-Hall, New Jersey (1963)
2. Wilkinson, J.H.: The Algebraic Eigenvalue Problem. Clarendon Press, Oxford (1965)
3. Kahan, W.: The Numerical Analyst as Computer Science Curmudgeon. https://people.eecs.berkeley.edu/~wkahan/Curmudge.pdf (2002)
4. Nazareth, J.L.: Numerical algorist vis-à-vis numerical analyst. Journal of the Cambridge Computer Lab Ring, Issue XXXIII, 8–10. www.cl.cam.ac.uk/downloads/ring/ring-2013-05.pdf (2013)
5. Knuth, D.E.: Selected Papers in Computer Science. CSLI Lecture Notes No. 59, Cambridge University Press, Cambridge (1996)
6. Braverman, M., Cook, S.: Computing over the reals: foundations for scientific computing. Notices of the AMS **53**(3), 318–329. Also available at https://arxiv.org/pdf/cs/0509042.pdf (1 Feb 2008) (2006)
7. Traub, J.F.: A continuous model of computation. Physics Today, 39–43 May 1999
8. Nazareth, J.L.: Numerical Algorithmic Science and Engineering. PSIPress, Portland, Oregon. Freely available at: http://www.math.wsu.edu/faculty/nazareth/NumAlg_19Jul12.pdf (2012)
9. Nazareth, J.L.: Real-number models of computation and HP-memristors: a postscript. http://www.math.wsu.edu/faculty/nazareth/Memristors.pdf (2014)
10. Gustafson, J.L.: The End of Error: Unum Computing. CRC Press, Boca Raton (2015)

11. Gustafson, J.L.: A radical approach to computation with real numbers. Supercomputing Frontiers and Innovations **3**(2), 38–53 (2016)
12. Gustafson, J.L., Yonemoto, I.: Beating floating point arithmetic at its own game: posit arithmetic. Supercomputing Frontiers and Innovations **4**(2), 71–86 (2017)
13. Cook, J.D.: Anatomy of a posit number. John D. Cook Consulting Blog. Available at: https://www.johndcook.com/blog/2018/04/11/anatomy-of-a-posit-number (2018)
14. Nazareth, J.L.: Computer Solution of Linear Programs. Oxford University Press, Oxford (1987)
15. Greenbaum, A.: IEEE floating point vs posits. SIAM News Blog. Available at https://sinews.siam.org/Details-Page/ieee-floating-point-vs-posits (2018)
16. De Dinechin, F., Forget, L., Muller, J-M., Uguen, Y.: Posits: the good, the bad and the ugly. CoNGA 2019, Singapore. https://hal.inria.fr/hal-01959581v3 (2019)
17. Nazareth, J.L.: Hierarchical implementation of optimization methods. In: Boggs, P., Byrd, R.H., Schnabel, R.B. (eds.) Numerical Optimization, 1984, pp. 199–210. SIAM, Philadelphia (1985)
18. Dantzig, G.B.: Linear Programming and Extensions. Princeton University Press, Princeton (1963)
19. Renegar, J., Shub, M., Smale, S. (eds.): Mathematics of Numerical Analysis. American Mathematical Society, Providence, Rhode Island (1996)
20. Moore, C., Mertens, S.: The Nature of Computation. Oxford University Press, Oxford (2011)
21. Nazareth, J.L.: Differentiable Optimization and Equation Solving: A Treatise on Algorithmic Science and the Karmarkar Revolution. Springer, New York (2003)
22. Nazareth, J.L.: An Optimization Primer: On Models, Algorithms, and Duality. Springer, New York (2004)
23. Press, W.H., Teukolsky, S.A., Vetterling, W.T., Flannery, B.P.: Numerical Recipes in FORTRAN: The Art of Scientific Computing, 2nd edn. Cambridge University Press, Cambridge (1992)
24. Solomon, J.: Numerical Algorithms: Methods for Computer Vision, Machine Learning, and Graphics, 1st edn., Sects. I–III. A.K. Peters, London (2015)
25. Nazareth, J.L.: On conjugate gradient algorithms as objects of scientific study. Optimization Methods and Software **18**, 555–565; **19**, 437–438 (an appendix) (2006)
26. Nazareth, J.L.: The Newton-Cauchy Framework: A Unified Approach to Unconstrained Nonlinear Minimization. Lecture Notes in Computer Science 769, Springer, Berlin (1994)
27. Nazareth, J.L.: DLP and Extensions: An Optimization Model and Decision Support System. Springer, Heidelberg (2001)
28. Nazareth, J.L.: DLPEDU: A Fortran-77 Open-Source Prototype Implementation of the DLP Optimization System, vii+207p. www.math.wsu.edu/faculty/nazareth/dlpedu-ebook.pdf (2017)
29. Nazareth, J.L.: A DLP Primer, 18p. www.math.wsu.edu/faculty/nazareth/Vineyard-DLP-Primer.pdf (2017)
30. Kahaner, D., Moler, C., Nash, S.: Numerical Methods and Software. Prentice-Hall, Englewood Cliffs (1989)
31. Greenbaum, A., Chartier, T.P.: Numerical Methods: Design, Analysis, and Computer Implementation of Algorithms. Princeton University Press, Princeton (2012)
32. Gowers, T., et al.: The Princeton Companion to Mathematics. Princeton University Press, Princeton (2008)
33. Chaitin, G.: Meta Math! The Quest for Omega. Pantheon, Random House, New York (2005)

GPSR Compliance
The European Union's (EU) General Product Safety Regulation (GPSR) is a set of rules that requires consumer products to be safe and our obligations to ensure this.

If you have any concerns about our products, you can contact us on

ProductSafety@springernature.com

In case Publisher is established outside the EU, the EU authorized representative is:

Springer Nature Customer Service Center GmbH
Europaplatz 3
69115 Heidelberg, Germany

www.ingramcontent.com/pod-product-compliance
Ingram Content Group UK Ltd.
Pitfield, Milton Keynes, MK11 3LW, UK
UKHW020239061126
16351UKWH00016B/56
9783031217630